Howard Pyle

Twayne's United States Authors Series

David J. Nordloh, Editor

Indiana University, Bloomington

TUSAS 514

Howard Pyle with daughter, Phoebe.
Courtesy of Delaware Art Museum, Howard Pyle Collections, Wilmington, Delaware.

Howard Pyle

By Lucien L. Agosta

Kansas State University

Twayne Publishers
A Division of G. K. Hall & Co. • *Boston*

For my father and mother,
Anthony and Louise Landes Agosta

Howard Pyle

Lucien L. Agosta

Copyright © 1987 by G. K. Hall & Co.
All Rights Reserved
Published by Twayne Publishers
A Division of G. K. Hall & Co.
70 Lincoln Street
Boston, Massachusetts 02111

Copyediting supervised by Lewis DeSimone
Book production by Janet Zietowski
Book design by Barbara Anderson

Typeset in 11 pt. Garamond
by Compset, Inc. of Beverly, Massachusetts

Printed on permanent/durable acid-free paper
and bound in the United States of America

Library of Congress Cataloging in Publication Data

Agosta, Lucien L.
  Howard Pyle.

  (Twayne's United States authors series : TUSAS 514)
  Bibliography: p. 158
  Includes index.
  1. Pyle, Howard 1853–1911—Criticism and interpreta-
tion. I. Title. II. Series.
PS2671.A36 1987   813'.4   86-25778
ISBN 0-8057-7493-9 (alk. paper)

Contents

About the Author

Lucien L. Agosta received his B.A. from Louisiana State University and his M.A. and Ph.D. from the University of Texas at Austin. He is an associate professor of English and Director of Composition at Kansas State University and has published articles on a variety of authors, among them the Brownings, Thornton Waldo Burgess, Thomas Hughes, Richard Wright, Kurt Vonnegut, and D. G. Rossetti.

Preface

Howard Pyle was a late nineteenth-century American artist, illustrator, and writer. His theories and the impact of his work revolutionized American illustration. With his students—among them N. C. Wyeth, Maxfield Parrish, and Jessie Willcox Smith—he formed the still-influential Brandywine school of American painting. According to Elizabeth Nesbitt, Pyle was also "the first truly great American author and illustrator of children's books," an assessment distilled from her earlier comments on Pyle in *A Critical History of Children's Literature:* "The period in which Howard Pyle did his work frequently has been spoken of as [a] Golden Age in children's literature. . . . It is difficult to do justice to his contribution to the shining quality of that era. The magnitude and diversity of his work elude definition."[1] This judgment is reinforced by the recent inclusion of two of Pyle's best works, *The Merry Adventures of Robin Hood* and *The Story of King Arthur and His Knights,* in the "Canon of Children's Literature" (1983), a list of sixty authors and titles compiled by the Children's Literature Association to include those works published before 1970 that are "of major literary merit" and/or feature "excellent illustration," and that "should be known by every adult specializing in the study of literature for children." Indicative of the enduring interest in Pyle as author and illustrator is the continuing market for his works: most of the books he wrote and illustrated for children have never been out of print, and many of them are currently available in multiple editions.

Yet in spite of these assessments and the viability of his works in the marketplace, Pyle has suffered an almost total critical neglect, even among students of children's literature and popular culture, a neglect occasioned, according to Perry Nodelman, by a persistent and unexamined preference for nineteenth-century British over North American writers for children. In his recent editorial on "Howard Pyle and the Adolescence of American Children's Literature" Nodelman records the excitement of his belated discovery of Pyle's works and concludes with the hope that scholars and general readers will soon "find it possible to admire Jacobs *and* Harris, Carroll *and* Baum, Stevenson *and* Pyle."[2] This book on Howard Pyle, the first to discuss his literary works at length and to demonstrate the interrelatedness of his illustrations and texts, aims at reintroducing a significant figure in American children's literature, one whose reputation has for too long been eclipsed.

The book is divided into five chapters, the first a biographical survey of Pyle's life and career and the last offering a summary assessment of his achievement. For purposes of clarity the three middle chapters are arranged according to genre rather than strict chronology. Chapter 2, for example, involves a critical consideration of Pyle's retellings of traditional narratives and legends, and includes an examination of his classic book on Robin Hood and his four-volume collection of Arthurian tales. Though the first and last works of his career, these books merit primary discussion because they give the best indication of Pyle's skill as storyteller and artist. *The Merry Adventures of Robin Hood,* acclaimed in both Europe and America when published in 1883, combines Pyle's most successful work in the verbal and visual arts. William Morris, a knowledgeable judge not only of illustration but of total book design, was incredulous that anything of such excellence could come from America's commercial presses. More recently, Zena Sutherland, Dianne Monson, and May Hill Arbuthnot have argued that though there are numerous versions of the Robin Hood tales now available for children, "the prose version by Howard Pyle, with his spirited illustrations, is the text they should know." Pyle's version "remains for generation after generation of children one of the most exciting narratives in all literature."[3] Though *The Merry Adventures of Robin Hood* is thought to be his best book, the four volumes of the Arthurian tales (1903–10), themselves modeled on the earlier *Robin Hood,* also accomplish that interdependence of text and illustration that characterizes Pyle's most successful work.

The third chapter discusses Pyle's illustrated collections of literary folk and fairy tales and his fantasy fiction. Pyle was one of the first Americans to write what are now known as literary folktales, a subgenre characterized by a transmutation of the plots, themes, and motifs of folklore into elaborated stories that obey literary rather than oral conventions and that are associated with particular writers and eras rather than with the anonymous folk. Pyle is linked with Charles Perrault, John Ruskin, Oscar Wilde, George MacDonald, and Hans Christian Andersen as having had a lasting influence on the form of the literary folktale. In this chapter a discussion of Pyle's three folktale collections, *Pepper & Salt* (1886), *The Wonder Clock* (1888), and *Twilight Land* (1895), precedes an examination of his two fairy-tale romances for adults, *A Modern Aladdin* (1892) and *The Price of Blood* (1899), both elaborations of folktale conventions. A look at Pyle's speculative myth, *The Garden Behind the Moon* (1895), concludes the chapter.

The same generic principle governs the organization of Chapter 4, an assessment of Pyle's historical fiction for children and a reconsideration of his now-neglected books of adventure and romance for adolescents and adults. The chapter begins with a discussion of Pyle's medieval historical novels for children, *Otto of the Silver Hand* (1888) and *Men of Iron* (1892), his best works in this genre. There follows an examination of his pirate adventure romances, significant examples of fin de siècle popular formula fiction. The chapter concludes with a consideration of *Rejected of Men* (1903), Pyle's only "realist" novel. In his popular historical fiction—characterized by well-constructed plots, plentiful action, and careful and authentic depictions of past places and times—Pyle experimented alternately with romantic and realist fictional conventions and thus embodied the two conflicting currents of late nineteenth- and early twentieth-century American fiction.

In writing this book, I am greatly indebted to Charles D. Abbott's 1925 biography of Howard Pyle, from which I gathered many of the details for the biographical first chapter, and to Henry C. Pitz's 1965 study of Pyle's life and dual art, which provided a helpful point of departure for my own critical judgments.[4]

From Kansas State University I received a 1984 Summer Faculty Research Grant and a sabbatical leave for 1984–85. Without this support I would have been considerably longer in completing this project. For his role as facilitator and for his continuous encouragement I would like to thank my department head, Professor Henry J. Donaghy; and for years of assistance in all manner of practical ways I owe a large debt to the English department's secretarial staff, especially Billie Tunison. To the staffs of the Boston Public Library, the Brandywine River Museum at Chadds Ford, Pa., the Delaware Art Museum at Wilmington, the Free Library of Philadelphia, and the Drexel University Library Archives, I extend my thanks for their generous assistance. Howard Pyle Brokaw, a grandson of Howard Pyle, offered me both useful information and excellent advice, for which I am grateful.

I especially appreciate the helpful criticism given me on this project by my Twayne editor, David J. Nordloh, and by my colleague, Phyllis Bixler. She suggested the project to me in the first place and sustained me through it. I cannot thank her enough.

Lucien L. Agosta

Kansas State University

Acknowledgments

Illustrations from Howard Pyle's works are reproduced courtesy of the following holders of the original drawings:

pages 40, 41	Print Collection, New York Public Library—Astor, Lenox, and Tilden Foundations.
pages 52, 72, 108, 117	Permanent Collections, Delaware Art Museum, Wilmington, Delaware.
page 77	frontispiece: Brandywine River Museum, Chadds Ford, Penn.; title page: Metropolitan Museum of Art, New York City.
pages 54, 59	Private collection of Mr. Howard Pyle Brokaw.
page 134	Private collector.
pages 86, 92	Whereabouts of the original drawings unknown.

Chronology

1891   Edits *The Buccaneers and Marooners of America.* 1 August, son Howard born.

1892   *Men of Iron; A Modern Aladdin.*

1894   Initiates teaching career, Drexel Institute, Philadelphia. 10 February, daughter Eleanor born.

1895   *The Garden Behind the Moon; Twilight Land; The Story of Jack Ballister's Fortunes.* 15 October, son Godfrey born.

1896   Appointed Director of School of Illustration, Drexel Institute.

1897   16 June, gives commencement address, Delaware College. Illustrations for Woodrow Wilson's *George Washington* exhibited at Drexel and at St. Botolph Club, Boston. 29 October, son Wilfrid born.

1898   First summer class at Chadds Ford, Pa., for ten Drexel scholarship students.

1899   *The Price of Blood.*

1900   14 February, resigns from Drexel Institute; opens Howard Pyle School of Art in Wilmington.

1902   June, delivers annual address at the Art School, Yale University.

1903   *The Story of King Arthur and His Knights; Rejected of Men.* Convenes last of the five Chadds Ford summer schools.

1904   Lectures at Art Students League, New York, every other Saturday until May 1905. Contributes campaign materials for Theodore Roosevelt.

1905   *The Story of the Champions of the Round Table.* Becomes art editor, *McClure's Magazine;* mural commission for *The Battle of Nashville,* Minnesota State Capitol; lectures at Chicago Art Institute. Prolific year in illustration.

1906   August, resigns from *McClure's.*

1907   *The Story of Sir Launcelot and His Companions; Stolen Treasure.* Paints mural, *The Landing of Carteret,* Essex County Court House, Newark, New Jersey. Elected member of National Academy of Design.

1908   *The Ruby of Kishmoor.*

1910   *The Story of the Grail and the Passing of Arthur*. Completes mural for Hudson County Court House, Jersey City, New Jersey. 22 November, sails for Italy to study murals.

1911   Dies 9 November in Florence.

Chapter One

A Portrait of the Artist

"The Bloody Quaker"

In a brief autobiographical sketch published posthumously in *Woman's Home Companion* Howard Pyle described a picture with text he had made at the age of eight, just at the outbreak of the Civil War. The picture represented a bandy-legged Zouave with baggy red breeches and Turkish fez holding a Union flag and striking with his sword at a cowering rebel. According to Pyle, "There was lots of smoke and bombshells in the picture, and a blazing cannon and an array of muskets and bayonets. . . . Accompanying this picture was a legend telling how the cannon-thunder roars, how the sword flashes in the air and falls upon the enemy of the nation. The text, I remember, concluded with the words, 'Ded! Ded! Ded is the cesioner!' (Secessionist! I was never a good hand at spelling.)"[1]

Commenting on the central paradox underlying this juvenile production, Pyle noted that "The picture and the poem are hardly of the pacific nature one would expect of a boy with two hundred years of pure Quaker blood in his veins, but I have always had a strong liking for pirates and for highwaymen, for gunpowder smoke and for good hard blows."[2] This ironic early proclivity for the raucous and the combative fueled a lifelong celebration in story and picture of pirates, knights, and medieval outlaws, and led certain of Pyle's youthful acquaintances aware of his pacifist Quaker antecedents to dub him "The Bloody Quaker."[3] In a number of his works for adolescents and adults—*Within the Capes,* "Captain Scarfield," and *The Ruby of Kishmoor,* for example—Pyle enjoyed probing this paradox by thrusting sober Quakers into the most violent and exotic of adventures, often involving pirates and desperadoes.

In his works featuring pirates, bandits, and knights Pyle explored the tensions between civilization and barbarism, law and license, social order and individual freedom. Drawing his heroes and adventurers from both sides of these dialectics, he admired those who foster civilization and was fascinated by those who subvert it. Among those works extolling the virtues of social order over individual freedom are Pyle's renditions of Arthurian romances and certain of his historical narratives and folktales. Pyle admired King Arthur, for example, for bringing independent and willful lords under a chivalric code intended to civilize the barbaric. Similarly, he applauded the extension of the Emperor Rudolph's civilizing rule over the lawless German barons in *Otto of the Silver Hand,* and in his folktales he often featured the successful social integration of his folk heroes.

With equal relish, however, Pyle drew strong portraits of those adventurers who undermine the social order, who, through their bravado and daring, resist civilizing influences and champion individual freedom. The pirate tales and the Robin Hood adventures fit into this class. Though Robin Hood reacts against a corrupt social order, his attractiveness results from his woodland existence free of the constraints imposed by society. For Pyle, pirates too provided "a little spice of deviltry," a "titillating twang to the great mass of respectable flour that goes to make up the pudding of our modern civilization." According to Pyle, pirates and outlaws and bandits appeal to the "unsubdued nature in the respectable mental household of every one of us that still kicks against the pricks of law and order." For Pyle, the pirate was attractive because of his "desperate courage" and "his battle against the tremendous odds of all the civilized world. . . ."[4] In his works, then, Pyle, the hereditary Quaker, features the often bloody conflict attendant upon the establishment as well as the subversion of social order. His heroes are men of action, and his works exhibit a fascination with both lawgivers and brigands.

Pyle's settled and relatively uneventful life, however, contrasts sharply with those lives of violence and romantic adventure chronicled in his works. His preference for the familiar and the domestic in his personal life insured that his own adventures were to be largely vicarious ones. N. C. Wyeth's tableau of Pyle enjoying a cozy domesticity even while apparently immersed in a world of imaginative experience is typical of the many reminiscences of Pyle penned by his students and acquaintances: "We saw through the high windows a sight which impressed me much. There was Mr. Pyle reading, his face of great character intently bent on a book, and flocked around the rest of the table were five of his children reading or drawing and on one side Mrs. Pyle with the youngest child in her lap and at her feet a cat and dog lay asleep."[5] According to Henry C. Pitz, Pyle's most recent biographer, it pleased Pyle to be taken not only as a family man but as "a prosperous man of business";[6] and in Henry Seidel Canby's autobiographical reminiscences of Wilmington, Delaware, in the 1890s, Pyle is classed with those other model citizens, "the local bankers," because "he belonged to a respectable Quaker family, held ultra conservative Republican opinions" (aired in the campaign materials he designed for Roosevelt and Taft), and was known "to earn an income which was considered fantastic in our town, considering what he did for a living."[7] Pyle used this large income to participate fully in Wilmington's upper middle-class social life, sponsoring in 1905, for example, a coming-out party for his daughter Phoebe to which Theodore Roosevelt and his wife sent arrangements of carnations and American Beauty roses. According to N. C. Wyeth, Phoebe Pyle's Wilmington debut in a five-hundred-dollar ballgown preceded similar parties in Boston and Washington.[8] In business, politics, and social life, then, Pyle seems to have accepted the prevailing upper middle-class social values.

In a letter to Edwin Austin Abbey, Pyle contrasted this quiet, respectable life in Wilmington with what he thought to be Abbey's more active, exciting life abroad: "I wonder whether two lives could be more different than yours and mine: the one full of go, novelty and change: the other humdrum, mossy, and—no, I will not say dull or stagnant, for it suits me to perfection. Yes, it suits me so perfectly that I doubt whether I shall ever cross the ocean to see those things which seem so beautiful and dream-like in my imagination, and which if I saw might break the bubble of fancy and leave nothing behind but bitter soapsuds."[9] In this passage Pyle makes it clear that his well-regulated, "humdrum" public life was relieved by an active imaginative life, which he fostered and protected. The "inner light" of his Quaker childhood took in adulthood the form of intense imaginative engagement in the realms of fantasy and romance. "You may never know what romantic aspirations may lie hidden beneath the most sedate and sober demeanor," he wrote in the first chapter of *The Ruby of Kishmoor,* a romance detailing the return of Jonathan Rugg, Pyle's alter ego, to the safety and sobriety of Philadelphia Quaker life after his violent, almost dreamlike adventures in Jamaica.[10]

As with *The Ruby of Kishmoor,* Pyle's works in art and literature are often imaginative explorations of a life from which he dwelt far removed. The tension between his public life and his inner imaginative life provides a perspective glass through which to view his career as writer, illustrator, and teacher.

"An Illuminating Joyfulness": The Early Years

Howard Pyle was born in Wilmington, Delaware, on 5 March 1853, the eldest son of Margaret Churchman Painter and William Pyle. His parents were of old Quaker stock, some of their forebears having arrived from England in 1682 aboard the *Welcome,* the first ship bringing Quaker immigrants to the Brandywine Valley. Though his parents were read out of Quaker meeting when Pyle was seven for their frequent attendance at a Swedenborgian church, Pyle's Quaker heritage and his strong attachment to the Brandywine Valley of his ancestors were of profound significance in determining the man he was to become.

An equally important determining factor was the influence of Pyle's mother, whose unfulfilled literary and artistic aspirations insured that her three sons and her daughter would be exposed to the best books and pictures that she could acquire. According to Pyle, his mother brightened his childhood with "an illuminating joyfulness in beautiful things."[11] She presided over an eighteenth-century fieldstone farmhouse from which Pyle could watch laden Conestoga wagons lumber into Wilmington on the Kennett Pike. Before the fireplace in winter and in the house's lovely old gardens during summer, Mrs. Pyle read with her children from European collections of folktales and a plentiful supply of illustrated novels by Dickens, Thackeray, Bunyan, and Defoe. In addition, she pored over the stories and illustrations in *Punch,* the *Illustrated London News,* the *Sunday Magazine, Cornhill,* and other illustrated papers of the time, exposing her children to the rich imaginative realms of such important British artists and illustrators of the 1860s as Arthur Boyd Houghton, Frederick Sandys, Charles Keene, John Leech, John Tenniel, and the Pre-Raphaelites—Rossetti, Holman Hunt, John Everett Millais, and later, Edward Burne-Jones. According to Henry Pitz, it was at his mother's knee that Pyle became accustomed to associating pictures with accompanying texts: "The dialogue between the literary and the pictorial was ingrained from the beginning."[12]

This early diet of illustrated books and magazines produced the desired effect on Howard and on his sister Katharine, who also later wrote and illustrated books for children. As Pyle himself testified, his predilections declared themselves at an early age. "I cannot remember the time," he wrote, "when I was not trying to draw pictures." The impulse to write had also come very early: in his autobiographical sketch for *Woman's Home Companion* Pyle recalled the day when, inspired to write a poem, he had actually put pencil to the paper his mother had supplied him before realizing that he was not yet able to read or write.[13]

Soon after the start of the Civil War the family leather business declined, necessitating the sale of the farmhouse and its gardens. After the family had settled in a smaller house in town, Howard was sent first to the Friends' School and then to a small private school conducted by Thomas Clarkson Taylor. In neither school did he excel, preferring to draw pictures on his slate rather than do sums. Pyle apparently learned less at school than at home where he had access to his mother's copies of Percy's *Reliques of Ancient English Poetry*, Ritson's collection of Robin Hood ballads, Malory's *Morte d'Arthur*, and various books of German folktales. These were to become the inspirations for the works for children on which his literary reputation still rests. In addition, he read avidly the illustrated newspapers of the day, especially *Frank Leslie's Illustrated Newspaper* and *Harper's Weekly*, for news and pictures of the war. The increasing demand of the American reading public during the war for illustrations of all kinds was greatly to influence American publishing history and consequently the directions taken by Pyle's artistic career.

At the age of fifteen or sixteen he was taken out of school and set upon a program of independent study designed to prepare him for entrance to a university. Not very long afterwards his parents yielded to the inevitable, gave up their expectations of his ever earning a college degree, and enrolled him in a small private school run by the Antwerp-trained artist, Van der Weilen, who was to provide Pyle with his only systematic training in art. For three years Pyle commuted from Wilmington to Philadelphia, where he endured the traditional academic regimen of precise copying from plaster casts and then from the posed model. At the end of three years he set up a studio at home and entered fully into the social life of his Wilmington contemporaries while helping his father in the leather business and trying to decide upon a career.

During nearly five years of uncertainty Pyle read widely, discovering Darwin, Trollope, Carlyle, and, most important, William Dean Howells, with whom he was later to enjoy a warm personal friendship as well as a professional relationship. Pyle's keen admiration for Howells was in many ways paradoxical. Howells was, after all, repudiating the prevalent nineteenth-century fictional form of the romance for more realistic portrayals of contemporary American life. Though Pyle applauded Howells's novels as the realization of a long-awaited form of indigenous American literary art, his own literary output would consist, with the notable exception of *Rejected of Men,* almost exclusively of romances, melodramas, and tales of wonder far removed in theme and in time and place from the late nineteenth-century American life so closely scrutinized by Howells and other American realists. In addition, Pyle's principal works were to draw almost entirely upon traditional European ballads, folk heroes, and folktale plot formulas. In short, the fictional types he so admired Howells for undermining, Pyle himself was soon to adopt as best suited to his ventures into the imaginative realms of adventure and romance.

At the end of this five-year gestation period, in spring 1876 Pyle, aged twenty-three, traveled to Chincoteague Island off the coast of Virginia to observe the annual roundup of wild ponies. There he made a number of illustrations and took notes he intended to use in a journal article. Shortly after his return to Wilmington, he submitted a verse with illustrations entitled "The Magic Pill" to *Scribner's Monthly.* Surprised by its prompt acceptance accompanied by a check, Pyle then sent a short tale to *St. Nicholas,* the most important magazine for children of that time. Encouraged by a second success, Pyle wrote the Chincoteague article and sent it to *Scribner's.* A third acceptance prompted his father to drop by the Scribner's offices when next in New York on business. There he met Roswell Smith, the editor, who persuaded the elder Pyle to send his son to New York. Under the misapprehension that Scribner's would give him work sufficient to support himself, Pyle left Wilmington for New York in mid-October 1876.

Once in New York, Pyle found that his expectations at Scribner's had been too sanguine and that he had to make connections with other publishers to place his work. He was eventually to look upon this as fortunate. An interview with Mary Mapes Dodge, editor of *St. Nicholas,* resulted in the acceptance of a number of animal fables and illustrations. Ever the dutiful son, Pyle wrote diary-letters home to his mother, addressing her with the Quaker "thee," detailing his daily activities, and reflecting upon his successes and disappointments. The letters reveal that he worked diligently during the day, but spent his evenings at the theaters.

Toward the end of the year Pyle faced a series of setbacks that made him question his ability to succeed as an illustrator. Dissatisfied with the way some of Pyle's drawings had reproduced in *St. Nicholas,* Mrs.

Dodge sent him to the engraving house to learn how to adjust his drawings for successful engraving on wooden blocks. At about the same time Scribner's art director was encouraging Pyle to enroll in a model class to improve his drawing. Pyle interpreted these suggestions as implicit judgments about his abilities. His letters home reflect his discouragement and growing indecision concerning which vocation—author or illustrator—he would follow. On 18 November 1876, for example, he rejected his mother's decided opinion that in spite of recent discouragements he should devote himself to illustration: "I think thee is mistaken and that by all means a literary life is the proper one for me."[14] But less than three weeks later he was considering a career in art once again, his mind changed by his success in the life class he was attending at the Art Students League. There he came to realize that successful illustration depended upon the animating power of the imagination and the illustrator's ability to go beyond the model, to interpret and create, not simply copy. To this realization Pyle was to attribute his eventual success as illustrator and teacher.

Early in 1877 Pyle met Charles Parsons, art director at Harper and Brothers, then the largest publishing concern in the country. Parsons was necessarily an astute judge of talent, having to insure a steady supply of illustrations for Harper's large book trade and especially for its diverse illustrated publications, the *Monthly, Weekly, Young People, Round Table,* and *Bazaar.* In many ways Pyle's association with the Harpers marked the real start of his professional career. He soon began to feel a part of the Harper staff, forming close friendships with such luminaries as Edwin Austin Abbey, Arthur B. Frost, Charles Stanley Reinhart, and other leading illustrators of the day.

Encouraged by Parsons to submit pictorial ideas, Pyle learned his craft rapidly but was not yet considered technically competent to complete his own drawings for publication. He was paid for ideas and preliminary sketches that were then finished by a more experienced house illustrator before being engraved. Chafing under this restriction, Pyle asked Parsons in late 1877 to allow him to finish, without handing it over to another illustrator, an "idea-sketch" entitled "A Wreck in the Offing," representing a man bursting into a coastal life-saving station from a howling storm and pointing out into the darkness to alert the rescuers who have risen abruptly from a game of cards. Though reluctant, Parsons agreed. According to Pyle's own account, he worked on the drawing for over six weeks, finding it impossible to satisfy himself. Finally reduced by the cost of models and living expenses to his last nickel, he was forced to deliver the drawing to Harper's. Its acceptance and publication as a double-page cut in *Harper's Weekly* for 9 March 1878 was the turning point in his career, as he himself realized.

After the acceptance of "A Wreck in the Offing," Pyle suddenly found himself, at twenty-five, in demand as an illustrator. On 29 February 1878 he wrote to his mother that "Work is beginning to roll in upon me at last, and at last I think I have 'struck pan.' My work is beginning to pay better too and I think before long I shall be able to pay off my debts to father *in toto*." In the same letter Pyle described some of the projects on which he was then engaged, particularly his two drawings "in illustration to a most excellent story of modern Spanish life" by Charles Carroll wherein a caballero, having offended his sweetheart in a fit of jealousy by penning a poetic lampoon of her, finally succeeds in winning her affections by sending her a casket containing a broken pen resting upon a sheet of paper marked with the word "Retribution" written in his blood. Beneath this paper is the caballero's severed right hand. "A very effective dénouement, I think," noted Pyle, revealing an early penchant for the sensationalism that characterizes certain of his later adult romances.[15]

During this period Pyle was building a reputation, solidifying important contacts with publishers, honing his skills in the model classes held at the Art Students League, and enjoying an active social life. Recognized as a significant talent, he was admitted to the companionship of the leading young illustrators of his day—the "young Olympians," as he called them. With his closest friends Abbey, Reinhart, and Frost, Pyle joined other promising young illustrators in the formation of an Art Students' Club devoted to the discussion of art and the consumption of beer and pretzels. Within two weeks of informing his mother of the existence of this club, he was writing to assure her that its members were all respectable and that the beer and pretzels were "a secondary object."[16]

It was not long, however, before Pyle's friends began to leave New York—Abbey to England, Reinhart to Europe, Frost to Philadelphia. Late in 1879, after spending three years in New York, Pyle too decided to leave, feeling that he had accomplished all he had set out to do there. His professional skills refined and tested, his work now finding a lucrative market, he returned to a top-floor studio in his parents' home in Wilmington with the assurance of Charles Parsons that the Harpers would send him enough work to keep him fully occupied.

"Ceaseless Industry": The Professional Years

Parsons was true to his word, supplying Pyle with opportunities to illustrate works dealing primarily with colonial American life. Pyle prepared himself for these assignments by reading extensively in American history, soon becoming the premier historical illustrator for a post-Civil War America intent on redefining itself as a unified nation. Pyle's historical illustrations were famed for accuracy of detail, even down to the precise number of buttons on the coats of Revolutionary War soldiers. In addition to illustrating historical works by others, Pyle began to write and illustrate his own articles for the Harpers. The first, appearing in the February 1880 *Harper's Monthly,* was a piece on the Bartrams of Philadelphia, early Quaker botanists who acquainted European scientists with the wild flora of America. "Bartram and His Garden" was followed in the January 1881 *Monthly* by "Old Time Life in a Quaker Town," a reconstruction of life in colonial Wilmington.

These pieces, and the works soon to follow, indicate that Pyle had resolved his earlier career indecision by becoming both writer and illustrator. In these historical journal pieces, however, his text is clearly a convenience upon which to hang the illustrations. His interest in American history remained keen throughout his career, causing Woodrow Wilson to request Pyle as illustrator of his most important historical works and earning Pyle the admiration of Theodore Roosevelt, with whom he became friends in 1904. "I have lived so long in our American past," wrote Pyle, "that it is like a certain part of my life. My imagination dwells in it and at times when I sit in my studio at work I forget the present and see the characters and things of these old days moving about me. . . ."[17] His ability thus to enliven the past enabled him to produce illustrations that helped to determine the historical consciousness of an entire generation of Americans.

Between increasing assignments for the Harpers, Pyle was working hard on the text and illustrations for *Robin Hood,* a book for children already several years in the planning. He was also enjoying a rich social life among young Wilmington Quakers no longer restricted by traditional religious prohibitions against drama, music, and pictorial art. His excellent tenor voice secured him an invitation to join the chorus of a young people's lyceum then rehearsing at the home of the Pooles, another old Quaker family. There Pyle met the eldest Poole daughter, Anne; by July 1880 they were engaged. After assuring himself of an adequate income by renewing lapsed connections with Scribner's and by getting the Harpers to agree to provide him with at least $2,500 a year, Howard Pyle and Anne Poole married in the Quaker way on 12 April 1881 with A. B. Frost as best man.

In the first year of his marriage Pyle produced over one hundred illustrations, evidencing that "ceaseless industry" he considered necessary for success in any profession.[18] He also illustrated two books intended for children—*Yankee Doodle* (in the Caldecott style) and *The Lady of Shalott* (in the style of Walter Crane)—as early experiments in mass color printing, the technology for which was still primitive in America. Disappointed by these first attempts at color reproduction, Pyle devoted himself to illustrating in pen and ink and eventually black-and-white oils. Later, when color reproduction was refined, he added rich color to his palette.

For a number of summers following their marriage, his family vacationed at Rehoboth Beach on the Delaware coast, where Pyle joined them on weekends. Here, several miles from the dunes at Cape Henlopen where pirates were said to have buried treasure, he developed that passion for pirates that was to permeate many of his fictional works and express itself on numerous canvases. The Pyles continued at Rehoboth with their growing family—five sons and two daughters were born to them between 1882 and 1897—until Pyle opened the first of his famous summer schools in 1898 at Chadds Ford in the Brandywine Valley.

The simultaneous publication in England and America of *The Merry Adventures of Robin Hood* in 1883, the same year he built his Franklin Street studio in Wilmington, brought to fruition the project Pyle had been working on since the New York days. His careful attention to every detail of printing, layout, format, and binding introduced the concept of "the beautiful book" in America and earned him the grudging praise of William Morris, who, according to Joseph Pennell, "thought up to that time . . . nothing good artistically could come out of America."[19] Though the book's price prevented it from becoming an immediate best-seller in spite of its laudatory reviews, its prefatory invitation to escape from the sobriety and seriousness of everyday life into the "mirth and joyousness" of the "land of Fancy" was soon widely accepted, establishing Pyle's enduring reputation as a classic author and illustrator for children, a pivotal figure in what has come to be called the "Golden Age of Children's Literature."*Robin Hood* was followed in 1885 by *Within the Capes,* an adventure novel narrated by an old Quaker, Tom Granger, who recollects two youthful years during which he was confronted with treachery, shipwreck, murder, and the finding of a fortune in Spanish gold. The diversity of Pyle's work during these years was remarkable. Not only was he illustrating a full complement of articles for Harper's and other houses, but he was also illustrating his own historical journal pieces, producing tales of adventure and romance for children and adults, and writing and illustrating numerous folktales.

At first Pyle's folktales were retellings of the traditional European tales he had loved so much as a child and that continued to divert him in adulthood. His first such tale, "Hans Gottenlieb, the Fiddler," for example, derived directly from Thorpe's *Northern Mythology.* In a letter of 26 November 1876 Pyle had written to his mother from New York that the tales in Thorpe "could be woven, with some shaping, into amusing and quaint stories by combining two or three of them together."[20] "Hans Gottenlieb" appeared in *St. Nicholas* in April 1877, initiating a succession of such tales published in that magazine and in *Harper's Young People.* By the time his first superbly illustrated collection of stories, *Pepper & Salt, or Seasoning for Young Folk,* appeared in 1886, Pyle was beginning to invent his own plots in addition to retelling traditional tales. In his preface he offered the collection as "a pinch of seasoning in this dull, heavy life of ours," an escape from "all the troubles, the labors, and the cares" into the "innocent jollity and mirth" of Fancy.

Pepper & Salt was followed in 1888 by a second collection of tales, *The Wonder Clock,* which Pyle considered his best book of fairy tales because of its greater subject variety and stylistic polish. Separating the twenty-four tales chimed in by the old Wonder Clock were verses contributed by Pyle's sister Katharine. The book was an instant favorite with his rapidly growing audience, and, according to Charles Abbott, Pyle's first biographer, continued to be immensely popular, selling six times as many copies in 1919, for example, as in the year following its publication.[21]

In addition to *The Wonder Clock,* Pyle published over two hundred illustrations in 1888, a year of many accomplishments. Two other books—*The Rose of Paradise* and *Otto of the Silver Hand*—appeared in that year also. Set in 1720 in the Mozambique Channel, *The Rose of Paradise* details the adventures of the quiet, sober Captain John Mackra who loses the fabulous ruby of the novel's title to the pirate Edward England and then with great difficulty retrieves it. *Otto of the Silver Hand,* published simultaneously in England and America and the first and best of Pyle's three historical books for children, is set in a medieval Germany ruled by ruthless robber barons. Through its perfect blend of prose and Düreresque pen drawings, *Otto of the Silver Hand* features the triumph of civilization and order over brutality and barbarism. Its honest depiction of cruelty and evil sets it apart from most other late nineteenth-century books intended for children.

During the remarkable five-year period from 1883 to 1888 Pyle published six books, four of them enduring masterpieces for children. Apparently realizing that his two novels of adventure and pirate romance—*Within the Capes* and *The Rose of Paradise*—did not equal his works for children in literary merit, Pyle and his wife sailed in 1889 for Jamaica so that he might familiarize himself with the Caribbean and thus authenticate his pirate tales and illustrations. Their trip was cut short by the sudden death at age seven of their firstborn son, Sellers. The Pyles were unable to return to Wilmington in time for his funeral. His death in their absence haunted them for the rest of their lives and apparently initiated the period of religious speculation and inquiry Pyle aired in his correspondence with William Dean Howells which began about this time.

Long an admirer of Howells's novels, Pyle finally met this author of realist fiction in New York at the Franklin Square offices of their publisher, Harper and Brothers. They soon discovered their mutual interest in Swedenborg and their common grief in each having lost a child. A long correspondence ensued during the early 1890s in which Pyle responded to Howells's religious doubts and speculations by reexamining his own religious beliefs. In a letter of 29 December 1890, for example, Pyle confessed that in his attempts to offer Howells certain "crutches of reasonings as had one time helped me in my stumblings," those "old, disused staves . . . broke down under me so that I fell almost into the slough myself." In this letter, however, he reaffirmed his belief that Swedenborg was "the Divinely inspired prophet—no; the *mouthpiece* of Jehovah" and that the Swedish mystic's obscure *Arcana Coelestia* was, "next to the Bible upon which it stands, . . . the greatest book that I have ever read." He encouraged Howells to read it, assuring him that it would relieve all his doubts.[22] Pyle was to draw upon the philosophical and theological speculation of this time in the writing of *The Garden Behind the Moon* (1895) and the early drafts of *Rejected of Men* (1903) as well as several short works, including "To the Soil of the Earth," accepted by Howells for the June 1892 issue of the *Cosmopolitan,* and "In Tenebras," published in *Harper's Monthly,* February 1894.

This correspondence also led Pyle to illustrate a series of Howells's poems for *Harper's Monthly* that was later collected in *Stops of Various Quills* (1895), poems overcast with a philosophical pessimism.

Pyle's religious introspection and innate mysticism were, however, too strongly allied with his powerful work ethic and unfailing business sense to remove him from the workaday world. From 1889 to 1892, when his philosophical speculations were apparently most intense, he published three books and produced hundreds of illustrations and articles for magazine and book publishers. In 1891 he edited *The Buccaneers and Marooners of America,* John Esquemeling's often reprinted seventeenth-century account of Caribbean piracy. In the year following he published *A Modern Aladdin* (1892), "an extravaganza in four acts" featuring delicate pen-and-ink drawings appropriate to a fanciful transposition of the Aladdin story to eighteenth-century France. That same year saw the publication of his second work of historical fiction for children, *Men of Iron,* the chronicle of Myles Falworth's maturation to knighthood and the eventual restoration of his family to wealth and honor. The novel's halftone illustrations, produced photographically from original black-and-white oils, helped to establish Pyle as the foremost American illustrator of those popular medieval works so much in vogue at the turn of the century.

"A Not Inglorious Success": The Teaching Years

Shortly before Pyle moved to New York in 1876 to begin his apprenticeship as an illustrator, he had placed a notice in Wilmington's evening newspaper offering "lessons in drawing, sketching and painting in oils" in "Room No. 8—Masonic Temple."[23] Apparently few students enrolled, if any. When he again offered to teach illustration almost twenty years later, he could not accommodate all of the students eager to enter his classes. By 1894, when he began to teach, Pyle was an acknowledged leader in what has come to be called the "Golden Age of American Illustration."

After eighteen years as a professional illustrator, Pyle had much to offer as a teacher. He brought to the classroom wide experience with a variety of artistic styles and media reflecting the changing tastes of his audience and the rapid technological innovations that continued to advance American printing during his lifetime. He was a master of pen drawing, evidencing at least two different pen techniques. The first, derived from the bold line of Dürer, Burgkmair, Cranach, and other masters of the medieval German and Renaissance Italian schools, was used for the illustrations in *Robin Hood, Otto of the Silver Hand,* the early folktale collections, and the later Arthurian books. Also used by the illustrators of the British Arts and Crafts Movement of the 1880s, this technique featured what Rowland Elzea described as a "basic curvilinear and dense Victorian decorative style."[24]

According to Henry Pitz, Pyle's second pen style stemmed from "the Impressionist painters' explorations into the study of light and their attempt to seize and fix transitory natural effects."[25] From the French illustrator Daniel Vierge, whom he had come to admire during his New York apprenticeship, Pyle adopted what Rowland Elzea has called the "taut, sketchy, fast-moving line" employed in his later collection of folktales, *Twilight Land,* as well as in numerous magazine illustrations.[26] Unlike the first pen style, with its strong decorative sense and insistence on formal patterning, this second style sought to capture the evanescent effects of shifting light and shadow characteristic of more realistic depictions.

Pyle could also offer instruction in oil painting. By the time he began his teaching career, halftone reproduction of oils had become sophisticated enough to insure consistently clear images, prompting him to alternate between pen and ink and black-and-white oil for his illustrations. After some tentative and often disappointing experiments with color reproduction during the 1890s, Pyle achieved success with his full-color illustrations for Erik Bogh's "The Pilgrimage of Truth," which created a sensation when they appeared in the December 1900 issue of *Harper's Monthly.* After 1900 Pyle and the publishers could skillfully meet wide public demand for color illustrations.

In deciding to teach, Pyle wished to do more than merely share with younger artists the skills he had so painstakingly acquired. Ever zealous to raise the standards of American illustration, he felt that the established art schools of his time, with their emphasis on copying from plaster casts, were turning out skilled technicians rather than imaginative artists. In addition, smarting at Europe's cavalier dismissal of American art, he crusaded for a native art characterized by American methods used to depict American subjects. Ironically, however, Pyle himself relied upon European styles and sources for many of his most successful pen drawings, though he apparently felt that his popular and innovative magazine illustrations of American historical subjects qualified him to help define a national art of illustration soon to be recognized for its energy and brilliance even in Europe. In 1902, eight years after the initiation of his teaching career, Pyle could write in his essay "Concerning the Art of Illustration" that "the only distinctly American Art is to be found in the Art of Illustration." Nowhere else but in America, he asserted, "are illustrations made so abundantly and so beautifully. I sometimes think that we are upon the edge of some new era in which the art of beautifying books with pictures shall suddenly be uplifted into a higher and a different plane of excellence."[27] As illustrator and teacher, Pyle was dedicated to bringing this new era into existence.

Believing that "pictures are creations of the imagination and not of technical facility," Pyle determined to offer his students what he felt they most needed: "the cultivation of their imagination and its direction into practical and useful channels of creation."[28] His conviction that intensive training in technical proficiency tended to subordinate originality and imagination led him to denigrate mere copying, the cramping regimen through which he had travailed under Van der Weilen and which underlay instruction in European and American art schools. Thus the cornerstone of Pyle's teaching became the fostering of imaginative invention.

According to R. W. Lykes, Pyle's teaching depended upon two principles of instruction: a fostering of what he called "mental projection" and an insistence on original composition.[29] Mental projection involved the ability to thrust the self imaginatively into a scene being depicted. Pyle prided himself on his ability to dwell in the American scenes he was illustrating: "My friends tell me," Pyle once remarked, "that my pictures look as though I had lived in that time."[30] "Project your mind into the subject until you actually live in it," he told his students; "Throw your heart into the picture and then jump in after it."[31] He also stressed original composition and the development of a pictorial sense; instead of teaching set academic compositional patterns, he expected his students to invent the appropriate original design configurations needed to suggest their artistic intentions freshly and powerfully to a viewer. Pyle considered his composition classes to be at the heart of his instruction, and his students concurred that the inspiration received during these sessions fueled their subsequent careers.

As Wilmington boasted no art schools, Pyle offered his services in 1894 to the Pennsylvania Academy of Fine Arts in Philadelphia, the oldest art school in the nation and one of the most prestigious. His offer was refused, Academy officials declaring that the school was devoted to instruction in the fine arts, which excluded illustration. Not long after, Pyle, then famous as a teacher, in turn declined a belated invitation to membership on the Academy faculty because of this initial rebuff. The first phase of his teaching career began when the recently opened Drexel Institute of Art, Science, and Industry made him a teaching offer, which he accepted, conducting a course in "Practical Illustration in Black and White" at 2:00 P.M. on Saturday afternoons during the 1894–95 academic year. The class enrolled over thirty students, many others were turned away, and Pyle became almost immediately the most celebrated instructor in Philadelphia, drawing students away from the more established art schools.

By the end of the 1895–96 academic year Pyle's course was nationally known; the work of his first students—including Violet Oakley, Maxfield Parrish, Jessie Willcox Smith, Elizabeth Shippen Green, and Walter Everett—was beginning to appear in national journals; and the Drexel administration had decided to expand the illustration class into a School of Illustration under Pyle's direction, noting that the results of his instruction "have been such as to warrant the Institute in extending considerably the scope of this branch of its work in the Art Department."[32] During 1896–97, then, Pyle commuted to Philadelphia for two full days of teaching a week instead of one, leaving Wilmington before sunrise and returning after sunset. In May 1897 the school held its first public exhibition of work produced during the academic year, and Pyle described the school in *Harper's Weekly* as "a not inglorious success."[33]

Remarkably, his teaching at Drexel did little to stanch the steady stream of writings and illustrations flowing from his studio in Wilmington. During his first year of teaching, 1894, he published well over one hundred illustrations and wrote the first draft of *Rejected of Men.* In 1895 he produced over 150 illustrations as well as three books and the highly praised paintings used in Woodrow Wilson's *George Washington,* published in six installments in *Harper's Monthly.* Pyle conferred repeatedly with Wilson about these illustrations, which, according to Charles Abbott, were "the most notable series of historical illustrations which had yet made their appearance in an American magazine."[34] Accompanied by a catalog in which Pyle described his muse as "extremely American in her Inclinations," the paintings were exhibited first at Drexel and then in 1897 at the St. Botolph Club in Boston.[35] They were subsequently purchased by a group of prominent Bostonians and donated to the Boston Public Library, where they hung for many years in the Children's Room.

Also during 1895 Pyle combined his interests in colonial America and in pirate lore to produce his third historical novel for children, *The Story of Jack Ballister's Fortunes,* first serialized in *St. Nicholas.* The novel features the kidnapping and sale of Jack to a Virginia planter whose daughter is captured by Edward Teach, better known as Blackbeard, and later rescued by Jack. In addition to this adventure novel Pyle published his last collection of folktales, *Twilight Land,* earlier serialized in *Harper's Young People.* His third book of 1895, *The Garden Behind the Moon,* represented a departure from his preceding works. A moving allegorical tale prompted by the death of Pyle's young son Sellers, *The Garden Behind the Moon* is a Swedenborgian speculation about spiritual maturation and the place in the next world of those who die out of this world prematurely.

In addition to becoming director of Drexel's School of Illustration in 1896, Pyle completed almost one hundred illustrations and continued to produce short fiction for magazines. In 1898 he attempted to repeat his success in illustrating Wilson's *Washington* by producing for *Scribner's Magazine* a set of illustrations for Henry Cabot Lodge's "The Story of the Revolution," and in the year following he published *The Price of Blood,* a melodramatic "extravaganza" set in 1807 New York and involving a young attorney in fantastic adventures set for him by mysterious agents from the far East.

During the 1890s, then, Pyle was at the height of his powers. Though his teaching did not seem significantly to diminish his prodigious output of illustrations and writings, it did make considerable demands on his time. Weary of coaching the many obviously untalented students who entered his large Drexel classes, he began to yearn for smaller groups of carefully selected students guaranteed to profit from his instruction. Accordingly, in 1898 he persuaded the Drexel administration to finance a summer school at Chadds Ford on the Brandywine to be taught by him without remuneration and to enroll ten scholarship students on stipends of one hundred dollars each. The first of Pyle's famous summer schools was a success in terms of work done, and he reported to Drexel authorities that "All the students have shown more advance in two months of summer study than they have in a year of ordinary instruction."[36] The 1899 summer school was equally productive, a number of students having placed with publishers the works they produced in the old Chadds Ford gristmill used as a studio.

Pyle increasingly encouraged his students to offer their illustrations to the publishers, with the result that his instruction remained free of the sterile taint of the academy, and his students often left his tutelage as established professionals. The artistic and social success of these two summer sessions, however, made him even more dissatisfied with his large Drexel classes. Accordingly, on 14 February 1900 he resigned from the Drexel staff.

The second phase of Pyle's career as a teacher began in 1900 when he decided to open his own art school in Wilmington and had three teaching studios added to the front of his own studio on Franklin Street. In a letter to Edward Penfield, then art editor at Harper's, Pyle wrote that he would not accept students deficient in any of the following criteria: "first of all, imagination; secondly, artistic ability; thirdly, color and drawing.[37] The students were thus to have completed basic technical training before admittance. They were also to pay their own expenses, Pyle's instruction being without remuneration. He intended to produce not just "illustrators of books," but also "painters of pictures," regarding "magazine and book illustration as a ground from which to produce painters."[38] In establishing his school, Pyle clearly intended to exercise a shaping influence on American art and illustration.

The Howard Pyle School of Art opened its new studios in September 1900 with twelve students, certain of whom had been with Pyle at Drexel, the others selected from hundreds of applicants from across the nation. Instruction was informal, except for the Monday evening composition classes, though students were expected to put in full days before their easels. Pyle's frequent visits to the student studios were eagerly awaited. All students were expected to attend a Saturday evening class for a discussion of pictures on a common theme drawn by all, including Pyle. Life in his little colony was not all work, of course. From all accounts, the students were high-spirited and easily drew a willing teacher into their sport.

Pyle resumed the Chadds Ford summer schools in 1901 to provide his students with the opportunity to paint nature firsthand in natural light. Freed from the restrictions of the studio, his students worked hard, but played too, many recalling these summer months as Edenic. In 1903 Pyle convened the last of the Chadds Ford sessions, bringing to an end what Henry Pitz has termed "one of the greatest outdoor classes in American art."[39]

In 1903 Pyle celebrated his fiftieth birthday at a medieval banquet attended by his students dressed as characters from his works. At fifty, his energies seemed undiminished. In addition to his teaching, he published numerous illustrations that year as well as *Rejected of Men* and

The Story of King Arthur and His Knights, two very different works prompted by the divergent American and European literary influences operating on him throughout his career. *Rejected of Men,* Pyle's only "realist" novel, is the story of Christ's life and death set in late nineteenth-century New York and told from the point of view of the Pharisees, depicted as contemporary American business and religious leaders. *The Story of King Arthur and His Knights* is, however, more representative of the Pyle canon in its celebration of the British folk hero chronicled by Malory and in its use of the British Arts and Crafts pen-and-ink illustrative style, which had had such great effect in *Robin Hood,* the success of which Pyle was attempting to duplicate in the Arthurian works. A determined advocate of all things American, Pyle ironically chose to feature European folk heroes like Robin Hood and King Arthur in his most ambitious works for children, even at a time when America was claiming or creating its own native folk heroes such as Daniel Boone, Davy Crockett, Pecos Bill, Slue-foot Sue, and Paul Bunyan. Because Pyle favored European folk heroes over American ones and preferred the often sensational romance over the "realist" novel as a literary form for his adult works, he contributed relatively little to the creation of an indigenous American literary art, in spite of the impact on American children's literature of his illustrated works for young readers.

Pyle's lifelong attempt to shape and influence American illustration, however, prompted a widening of his teaching efforts during the first decade of the new century. During the winter of 1904–05, for example, he commuted to New York every two weeks to teach at the Art Students League, where he himself had taken lessons during his New York apprenticeship. Though disappointed in the caliber of most of the students, he nevertheless attracted a number of promising young artists to his school in Wilmington. After he was invited to give a lecture series at the Art Institute of Chicago, even more students flocked to Wilmington to study with the master, who was reiterating in Chicago his persistent belief that the young American artist "is overshadowed by the technical accumulation of foreign education, which . . . does not lend itself to the fulfillment of a characteristic American Art."[40]

In 1905 Pyle ceased teaching formal classes, preferring to offer advice and criticism privately to former students as well as to more established professional illustrators who were attracted in increasing numbers to Wilmington by Pyle's fame. With their influx, Wilmington was becoming one of the most important centers of illustration in the country; and Pyle, now in the third phase of his teaching career, found himself refining the skills of already accomplished illustrators rather than shaping talented novices into imaginative artists. He continued to critique the work of young illustrators privately and in a weekly criticism session until his departure for Italy in 1910.

During his sixteen-year teaching career Pyle's tutelage extended to almost two hundred students, among them an astonishing number of the succeeding generation's most important illustrators and teachers of illustration, including Stanley M. Arthurs, Harvey Dunn, Walter H. Everett, Elizabeth Shippen Green, Thornton Oakley, Maxfield Parrish, Frank Schoonover, Jessie Willcox Smith, and N.C. Wyeth. Most of Pyle's students acknowledged his seminal influence on their careers. Thornton Oakley, for example, credited Pyle with providing him the initial inspiration underlying his eventual success as artist and teacher. "We never heard one word from our beloved teacher concerning tools and methods," wrote Oakley; "His utterances were only of the spirit, thought, philosophy, ideals, vision, purpose."[41] Maxfield Parrish agreed, citing Pyle's ability to inspire his students as his greatest gift as a teacher: "It was not so much the actual things he taught us as contacts with his personality that really counted. Somehow, after a talk with him you felt inspired to go out and do great things, and wondered by what magic he did it."[42] N. C. Wyeth, too, wrote of Pyle's ability to make his pupils see life and art in a new way. In a 1902 letter to his mother Wyeth described his first composition lecture from Pyle as having "opened my eyes more than any talk I ever heard." Though later ambivalent about Pyle's teaching methods and his persistent influence on his art, Wyeth echoed the sentiments of most other Pyle students when he acknowledged his "profoundly deep sense of gratitude" to Pyle for his "years of friendship and guidance," resolving that in his own art he would "carry on the honest impulses [Pyle] awakened within us."[43] Able to inspire and direct a whole generation of illustrators, Howard Pyle must be reckoned one of the most significant art educators in the history of American art.

"Limitless Ambition of Purpose": The Late Years

Freed from organized classes for the first time in more than a decade, Pyle began to explore new career ventures, though he continued to write and illustrate, publishing almost two hundred illustrations in 1905 as well as his second volume of Arthurian tales, *The Story of the*

Champions of the Round Table. In 1905 he turned his attention to mural painting, then becoming increasingly popular as architectural embellishment in America's public buildings. To prepare for this new phase of his career, he painted seven allegorical mural panels in his home before accepting a commission to paint *The Battle of Nashville,* a mural completed in 1906 for the governor's reception room of the new Minnesota State Capitol.

Mural painting was not the only new venture for Pyle at this time, however. In late 1905 he accepted a half-time appointment as art editor for *McClure's Magazine* at a salary of $18,000. Apparently S. S. McClure hoped that Pyle would be able to persuade his students to submit their increasingly popular work exclusively to *McClure's* rather than to competing magazines. There is evidence that Pyle as editor made unreasonable demands on some of his former students, alienating several for a period. N. C. Wyeth, for example, was pressured to contract half of his time with *McClure's* and to hurry his other commissions, but angrily refused, accusing Pyle of using him for his own personal betterment. After five or six months Pyle admitted failure, his first in a long, successful career, and resigned from *McClure's,* hastening to mend the breaches with his former students.

Pyle returned to his heavy illustrating and writing commitments following the fiasco at *McClure's,* publishing in 1907 *The Story of Sir Launcelot and His Companions* as well as *Stolen Treasure,* a collection of the best of his pirate stories originally published in various magazines. That same year he painted *The Landing of Carteret,* a historical mural for the Essex County Courthouse in Newark, New Jersey, and was elected a member of the National Academy of Design. In 1908 he published his last romance, *The Ruby of Kishmoor,* and completed numerous magazine illustrations.

But Pyle was growing increasingly impatient at this time with what he judged to be the medieval and historical hackwork he was being asked to illustrate for the magazines. "I am in great danger of grinding out conventional magazine illustrations for conventional magazine stories," he complained to his editors at the Harpers in 1907.[44] After producing nearly three thousand illustrations for magazines and for over one hundred books by many of the leading British and American novelists, historians, and poets of the age, Pyle apparently felt that he was beginning to repeat himself. Though he continued to illustrate and to work—with decreasing vigor—on his last volume of Arthurian tales, *The Story of the Grail and the Passing of Arthur* (1910), he began to turn more and more to mural painting as a fresh creative outlet and as a way of meeting his increasing financial obligations. Thus, toward the end of his life he entered another phase with that "limitless ambition of purpose" he felt necessary for success in any profession.[45]

His most ambitious mural project, five historical panels for the Hudson County Courthouse in Jersey City, New Jersey, was completed in 1910. Recognizing that he was not yet able to solve the unique artistic problems posed by large wall decoration, he turned for answers to Italy with its long mural tradition as an economical place where he might spend a year studying the masterpieces of mural design and perfecting his own technique. Thus determined to confront at last the European artistic tradition he had so long attempted to evade in his struggle to create an indigenous American art, Pyle, age fifty-seven, set sail for Italy on 22 November 1910, accompanied by his family and his secretary, Gertrude Brincklé.

Ill when he left New York, his poor health persisted throughout the voyage. His reaction to Italy was ambivalent, apparently depending upon the vagaries of his deteriorating physical condition. Sick and unhappy in Rome, he soon went on to Florence, which he thought "wonderful" but "dirty and ramshackle compared to our American ideals." During his stay in Italy Pyle missed the comfort and security of the Wilmington home he had so rarely left. Southern Italy impressed him as "a great big charnel house, full of the dead and chiefly of the dead bones of the past," though in improved health he found himself admiring the Old Masters for a use of color "so remarkable that I do not see how any human being painted as they did." "I kept thinking of my pupils and wishing that they could see these pictures," wrote Pyle, apparently reversing his often-repeated dictum that European art had little to teach American artists and illustrators.[46]

Though debilitating bouts of "renal colic" prevented Pyle from working on the articles and illustrations he had hoped to produce while abroad, he did complete in Florence for the DuPont Company a large historical canvas—his last, as it turned out. For this painting he returned to the familiar and beloved Brandywine Valley for his subject—a train of Conestoga wagons loaded with gunpowder milled along the Brandywine River during the War of 1812. This last example of the decidedly American art for which Pyle was so famous was, however, suffused with a rich golden light, a long-delayed homage to the Italian Renaissance painters whose works he had so belatedly come to admire.

Soon after the completion of this canvas, Howard Pyle's health began to deteriorate alarmingly. On 9 November 1911 he died in Florence of Bright's disease. His burial in foreign soil was an ironic coda to the life of a man celebrated for his enduring contributions to American children's literature, devoted to the creation of a characteristic American art, and recognized as the premier illustrator and teacher in what has come to be called "the Golden Age of American Illustration."

Chapter Two

Tradition and the Individual Talent: Robin Hood and King Arthur

Howard Pyle's first work, *The Merry Adventures of Robin Hood* (1883), and his last, the four-volume Arthuriad (1903–10), blend late nineteenth-century sensibilities with the timeless fascination of the traditional legends and ballads.[1] Robin Hood steps forth in Pyle's work vaunting all of the anarchic high spirits essential to the original ballad Robin, but cleansed of his proclivities toward ribaldry and violence, a hero at home both in Sherwood Forest and in the Victorian nursery. King Arthur, too, reigns in Pyle's works with all the heroic magnanimity celebrated in the ancient sources, but, like Tennyson's Arthur, he also embodies the virtues requisite for the late nineteenth-century Anglo-American gentleman. Thus Pyle's two traditional heroes, stamped with his individual talent, embody timeless values at the same time that they endorse contemporary ones. In these works the past is "altered by the present as much as the present is directed by the past," a mark for T. S. Eliot of the enduring work of literary art.[2]

Though both works reflect Pyle's acute sense of the timeless and of the temporal, they differ markedly in attitude and atmosphere. *The Merry Adventures of Robin Hood*, the work of a young man, celebrates a rebel yeoman leader and his youthful high jinks in the forest. For Robin Hood, nature and the wilderness are refuge and asylum; outside of the greenwood is treachery and accident, faithlessness and intrigue. By contrast, the Arthurian volumes, the work of an older man firmly established in the world, portray a responsible aristocratic legislator imposing order and stability on his realm. In his Arthuriad Pyle repeatedly demonstrates, especially in his treatment of Launcelot, the dangers of attempting to remain in the youthful Arcadian realm of freedom from adult responsibilities celebrated in *Robin Hood*. The central unifying image in Pyle's history of Arthur is the distant castle, the vista of nurtured valleys after the woods have been cleared. Civility is in the walled cities to which the knights centripetally repair; forests are, for the most part, places of sudden and violent meetings, locales of enchantment, mystery, and madness.

Perhaps Pyle's fascination with these two seemingly disparate heroes results from a psychical affinity between them and himself. Granted their essential differences, Robin Hood and King Arthur nevertheless have in common their coteries of loyal and admiring disciples ever striving to imitate them. Certainly Pyle's own charismatic life was dedicated in large measure to imparting to similar coteries the ideals of art and the life of the artist that inspired his own career. Like Robin Hood, he gathered a high-spirited band around him for five idyllic summers of work and play in the Arcadian greenwood of the Brandywine Valley, summers many of his students were to remember as the high points of their lives. Like Arthur, too, he was the center of a court of loyal disciples who gathered at studios built for them in Wilmington, an artistic Camelot, where they learned not only the technical skills but, more important, the ideals necessary to dedicate themselves to productive lives as artists, for Pyle one of the noblest of callings.

Since *The Merry Adventures of Robin Hood* and the four-volume Arthuriad offer the best indication of Pyle's skill as storyteller and artist, they deserve primary consideration in any discussion of his works. Traditional tales refashioned with a vigor, a generosity of spirit, and a never-failing good humor, they continue to delight the contemporary reader even in an age when overt didacticism and deliberate archaism find little favor. Their continued availability in print in multiple editions and their inclusion in the "canon" of required reading recently compiled by the Children's Literature Association testify to their enduring popularity.[3]

The Merry Adventures of Robin Hood (1883)

First a yeoman hero of medieval ballad, then a Lord of Misrule rioting over sixteenth-century May Games, later elevated by Elizabethan dramatists into respectable courtly circles as the dispossessed earl of Huntingdon, and finally delighting children and the unlettered by his anarchic brawlings with butchers, tanners, and other artisans in seventeenth- and eighteenth-century chapbooks, Robin Hood had already appeared in many guises before his refashioning by Howard Pyle and other nineteenth-century Romantic writers. This reformation of Robin Hood had been prepared for in the previous century by the publications

of Thomas Percy's *Reliques of Ancient English Poetry* (1765) and especially Joseph Ritson's *Robin Hood* (1795), in which Ritson not only
provided reliable source material for a Robin Hood revival but also a
new mask for Robin to wear into the new century. A Jacobin admirer
of the French Revolution, Ritson transformed the medieval bandit into
a revolutionary guerrilla fighter, "a man who, in a barbarous age, and
under a complicated tyranny, displayed a spirit of freedom and independence, which has endeared him to the common people, whose cause
he maintained."[4] Following Ritson's lead, Sir Walter Scott initiated
the great nineteenth-century vogue for Robin Hood by casting him as
a Saxon champion against Norman oppression in *Ivanhoe* (1819).

This new Romantic guise, however, was not in itself sufficient to
remake Robin Hood into a viable hero able to speak to the concerns of
an increasingly industrialized nineteenth century, as Keats recognized
in his nostalgic "dirge for a national legend," wherein he laments that
Robin's "days have hurried by" and "All are gone away and past."[5] As
Dobson and Taylor demonstrate in their excellent history of the Robin
Hood legend, none of the numerous nineteenth-century poets and novelists who wrote about the outlaw of Sherwood Forest—Scott, Peacock,
Keats, Leigh Hunt, Tennyson, or Pyle—"proved able to make Robin
Hood seem relevant to the issues of [their] own day." Instead, Robin
and his carefree existence in the greenwood became for the nineteenth
century a focus for escapism and nostalgia, a pastoral oasis in the midst
of a world radically transformed by the Industrial Revolution. Thus,
according to Dobson and Taylor, "The writers of the Romantic period
and after popularized Robin Hood only at the cost of converting him
from a real outlaw into a literary symbol of a vanished and largely
illusory medieval Arcadia."[6]

Sharing the inclinations of his contemporaries, Pyle too set his Robin Hood to revel in a nostalgic Golden Age, a time out of time. In his
preface Pyle invites his readers to escape into a "land of Fancy," a "No-
man's-land" clearly demarked from the "every-day life" through which
we must "plod amid serious things."[7] The locus for the adventures is
an Arcadian greenwood "wherein no chill mists press upon our spirits,
and no rain falls but what rolls off our backs like April showers off the
backs of sleek drakes" (viii). "The sweet shades of Sherwood" (22) provide a pastoral retreat where the merry men—sometimes referred to as
"boys" (9)—suffer "neither care nor want" (1) and where, according to
Robin, "misfortune cometh not upon us" (22). In the greenwood those
who "dwelt apart from other men" pass their time in "games of archery

or bouts of cudgel play" (1) and "shoot the dun deer," a beneficent
nature never failing to feed them "upon venison and sweet oaten cakes,
and curds and honey" (22).

Robin's merry Arcadians are without wives, families, property, jobs,
or responsibilities. Their frequent disguises indicate that they are without defined roles, that they are protean, ever in the process of becoming. Sexuality remains adolescent, even prepubescent: Robin thinks
tenderly of Maid Marian on occasion, but she never appears; Little John
carries on several adolescent flirtations of short duration; and though
Allan a Dale marries Ellen in part 4 of the adventures, she disappears,
only to be mentioned once again in the epilogue. Women have no place
in this Arcadia, with the exception of the motherly Queen Eleanor and
the *femme fatale* Prioress of Kirklees at whose hands Robin meets his
death by treachery. In short, Robin Hood's is a boy-world, a Peter Pan
never-never-land removed from the adult world of work, marriage, and
responsibility.

Pyle uses every artistic means at his disposal to distance his readers
from the real world and entice them into a fanciful pastoral realm. In
his preface he admits to blurring the historical period that serves as
setting for Robin's adventures so that we will be unable to recognize
the "good, sober folks of real history"—Henry II, Eleanor of Aqui-
taine, Richard the Lion-Hearted—"but for the names tagged to them"
(vii). Pyle not only disavows historical authenticity, but he also endows
his characters with a language no longer spoken, if indeed it ever had
been, a language spiced with metaphor and richly textured poetic
rhythms, and studded with archaisms which, though they serve to
separate us from the everyday world, nevertheless too often prove dis-
tracting to contemporary readers, especially children. His detailed illustrations, too, emphasize that this is a realm other than the world of
prosaic experience: their heavy decorative borders bar immediate entry
into this realm, providing us instead with the frames through which
we glimpse the terrain and inhabitants of a land existing outside real
time and space, an imaginative realm of childhood to which we are
granted access only through the arts of picture and prose.

The genial minstrel-narrator of the preface, who serves as our guide
through this Land of Fancy, lifts "the curtain that hangs between here
and No-man's land." "Will you come with me, sweet Reader?" he asks.
"Give me your hand" (viii). Appropriately, the narrator's free hand is
depicted in the preface tailpiece holding aside a curtain for us to pass
into a sunlit realm where a road stretches to the horizon. This road

provides a central unifying image for the work: most of Robin's adventures occur as he wanders "through highway and byway" (5), along "broad Watling Street or the Foss Way" (915), and down the high roads stretching "white and dusty in the hot summer afternoon sun" (219). At the same time, the road figures as a metaphorical road of life down which Robin travels during the course of the narrative from his first becoming an outlaw to his eventual death by treachery. The minstrel-narrator guides us along this road until at the grave of Robin "we turn, each going his own way" (296). The illustrations, too, reflect this central unifying motif: most of the chapter headpieces and a number of the full-page cuts feature a road winding away from the central scene toward a distant horizon.

The array of characters and adventures encountered along the way are, according to the narrator, "all bound by nothing but a few odd strands of certain old ballads (snipped and clipped and tied together again in a score of knots)"(vii). Pyle, however, faced a more onerous artistic task than a mere cutting and pasting when he integrated these ballads into a continuous narrative frame and adapted them—coarse, bloody, and violent as they so often are—for a youthful audience. Because motives are rarely provided for human actions in the ballads, and because the sequence of cause and effect often remains tenuous, the original Robin Hood ballad narratives amount to little more than what Maurice Keen calls "a chain of accidents whose links constitute the episodic life-story of a conventional figure."[8] In his continuous though episodic narrative Pyle clarifies the logic, causal connections, and character motivations so conspicuously absent from the ballad tradition and, for the benefit of his youthful audience, transforms Robin from the often cruel, desperate, and bloodthirsty renegade/buffoon depicted in the ballads to a buoyant, virile, and consistently sympathetic youth ranging freely and merrily along the roads of an English North Country Arcadia. More than a mechanical splicing of the old ballads, *The Merry Adventures of Robin Hood* is a classic retelling of the traditional Robin Hood story and bears the stamp of Pyle's artistic individuality.

The adventures.   The work consists of a prologue, eight parts, and an epilogue. Each of these divisions, though woven into a chronological frame by the narrator's frequent summaries and forecasts and by adroit internal references to previous adventures, is thematically independent, apparently reflecting Pyle's original intention to publish the adventures serially. For example, the prologue, first published in *Harper's Young People*, is a brief bildungsroman, a sketch of Robin

Hood's evolution from hot-headed youth to responsible leader and lawgiver.[9] Pyle's interweaving of several traditional ballads in this prologue to recount how Robin was outlawed, gathered his band around him, and gained his right-hand man, Little John, bears close scrutiny as it typifies his use of traditional sources throughout the work. True in plot outline to the account in the Ritson ballad of how Robin came to be outlawed, Pyle nevertheless expurgates much of that ballad's extreme violence so as to begin his refashioning of Robin Hood's character even in the initial pages of the book.[10]

On his way to Nottingham to shoot in the sheriff's match, Robin encounters a group of fifteen foresters who taunt him about his youth. When the foresters menace him after his victory in a shooting wager set to prove his prowess and assuage his wounded pride, the ballad Robin, smiling with malice, calmly slays fourteen of the foresters before shooting their fleeing ringleader with an arrow "That split his head in twain." The ballad Robin then becomes a veritable engine of destruction when the villagers come out to capture him before his escape into "the merry green wood": "Some lost legs, and some lost arms, / And some did lose their blood."[11] Pyle's conception of Robin Hood, however, diverges significantly from the ballad. In the altercation following Robin's winning the wager, the chief forester, his head "spinning with ale," shoots an arrow, missing Robin's head by a scant three inches. Only then, in self-defense, does Robin return a shot, killing the treacherous forester. Stricken with grief, Robin's "heart was sick within him" as it was "borne in upon his soul that he had slain a man" (4). Pyle's Robin, mindful of this slaying in self-defense throughout his subsequent adventures, learns to avoid wherever possible situations that make bloodshed inevitable, a strategy which in large part accounts for his long reign in Sherwood. Whereas the balladeer maintains a morally neutral stance to Robin's excessive violence, Pyle clearly indicates that his Robin, though he reacts in relative moderation, is morally culpable for acting in haste and out of pride. Thus, at the outset, Pyle's indebtedness to the ballad tradition for basic plot situations is made clear, though his conception of Robin Hood's character remains fundamentally his own.

After the gathering of Robin's band, consisting of men outlawed for killing the king's deer in hunger or for having been despoiled of their inheritances by rapacious barons and rich abbots, the merry men bind themselves to a code intended to rectify, through guerrilla warfare, the social injustices that have made them victims. "They vowed that even as they themselves had been despoiled they would despoil their oppressors," taking from them what had been "wrung from the poor by unjust taxes, or land rents, or in wrongful fines" (15). This code provides a moral justification for the deeds of Robin's men and insures a more equitable distribution of wealth and individual rights for the common man, tenets dear to the heart of the work's democratic American author. In addition, the merry men vow to practice the usual chivalric deference to women, children, and the needy and defenseless. Thus, at the beginning of his work, Pyle provides for Robin and his band a higher social and moral code than the one they will so consistently defy throughout their adventures. Their lawlessness is redeemed by their devotion to a higher law.

In the prologue's conclusion Robin Hood acquires Little John as his lieutenant. Pyle follows his ballad source (Ritson 2, ballad 21) closely in featuring the famous quarterstaff confrontation on the bridge, even to incorporating some of the ballad's phrasing. However, apparently not content to leave the tale with the ballad Robin's soggy defeat and Little John's easy induction into the band, Pyle deviates from his source by having Little John refuse to join with one whose prowess is inferior to his own. Not until Robin bests him in a near-miraculous display of archery does Little John offer Robin his fealty. In thus adding an episode to the original ballad, Pyle underscores Robin's fitness to lead, a questionable attribute in much of the ballad tradition, where Robin apparently suffers too many ignominious beatings at the hands of pinders, tinkers, and beggars to qualify as a hero for Pyle. By the end of the prologue, however, Pyle has refashioned the ballad Robin into a hero whose engaging honesty and exceptional valor fit him for responsible leadership and make his subsequent adventures worthy of our attention.

Part 1 of the adventures involves a thematic integration of three separate ballads to show Robin's ingeniousness in negotiating the increasingly perilous traps set for him by the Sheriff of Nottingham, who, failing to take Robin by legal summons for the killing of his kinsman the forester, resorts to guile and then to force. In the first adventure the sheriff hires a dull-witted tinker from a neighboring village, the only one he can find foolhardy enough to serve Robin with a warrant. Robin's clever outwitting of the tinker at the tavern comes almost unchanged from the ballad source (Ritson 2, ballad 7), but in order to strengthen the heroic depiction initiated in the prologue, Pyle spares Robin the beating he later receives at the tinker's hands in the original ballad, having instead the tinker admit that Robin has won the contest of wits as well as of arms. With the failure of legal coercion, the sheriff tries guile, arranging the famous shooting match at Nottingham handily won by Robin in disguise. Pyle's elaborate descriptions of the prowess of individual archers as well as of costumes and class characteristics are reminiscent of Scott's descriptions of the famous tournament at Ashby-de-la-Zouche in *Ivanhoe*.

When guile fails, the sheriff resorts at last to force, capturing Will Stutely, rescued (as in Ritson 2, ballad 15) by the band just before being hanged. In this adventure Pyle explains how Will came to be captured, antecedents ignored by the balladeer, and reiterates, no less than three times, Robin's aversion to bloodshed: "Once I slew a man," says Robin, "and never do I wish to slay a man again, for it is bitter for the soul to think thereon" (34). To this aversion, according to the narrator, the sheriff and half of his men owed their lives. Part 1 ends with the sheriff's realization that to harass the wily and dangerous outlaws of Sherwood is to court disaster.

Part 2 of the adventures features Robin's revenge against the sheriff and integrates two traditional ballads, both of which depict the outlaw as a chameleon master of disguise, a liminal man of many masks, a trickster whose marginal relation to his society frees him to adopt any guise he wishes or accept any role foisted on him by others. In the first adventure of part 2 Robin buys the cart and wares of a butcher and travels to Nottingham where he sells meat to the "bonny lasses" for a kiss until he is assigned the role of "prodigal spendthrift" and invited to dine at the Butchers Guild. There the disguised Robin, outlaw-*qua*-butcher-*qua*-gull, taunts the sheriff about Robin Hood's winning the earlier shooting match, one of the many ways Pyle weaves this tale to the adventures related in part 1, and then tricks the avaricious sheriff into riding into Sherwood with 300 pounds to buy a herd of "horned beasts" valued at well over twice that amount. After his ordeal in Sherwood, the sheriff is required to pay his reckoning, not only for the evening's entertainment at the "merry inn" where Robin plays innkeeper, but also for the sheriff's treachery as featured in part 1. The double score settled, the sheriff is allowed to ride forth as an exemplum for the narrator's concluding moral tag about the folly of men who "overreach themselves through greed and guile" (56). Pyle's didactic ending of the tale differs markedly from the ballad conclusion (Ritson 2, ballad 5) where Robin dismisses the sheriff with an indirect but seemingly lewd suggestion about the sheriff's wife.

The further adventures chronicled in part 2 also display the outlaw's protean nature, which so fascinated Pyle. Little John's six-month service in the sheriff's household disguised as "Reynold Greenleaf" ends in Little John's stealing both the sheriff's cook and his silver plate. In the ballad ("A Lytell Geste of Robyn Hode," Ritson 1) Robin welcomes both cook and treasure, though in Pyle's version, Robin scolds Little John for stealing "like some paltry thief" from a man who has already "paid his reckoning" and who lately "hath done nought that we should steal his household plate from him" (74). When the credulous sheriff is once again beguiled into Sherwood by Reynold Greenleaf's account of having seen "a young hart all in green from tip to toe" (75), the ballad Robin humiliates the sheriff before forcing him to promise that he will no longer molest the merry men. The theft and the sheriff's humiliation, however, insure that this promise will soon be broken. Pyle's Robin Hood, on the other hand, is more generous in his attempt to mend relations with the sheriff: he tacitly offers a truce by returning the sheriff's stolen plate and escorts the sheriff out of Sherwood with his dignity intact. Thus our sympathies are completely with Pyle's Robin and against the sheriff who treacherously repudiates the proffered truce.

The delightful variations on the themes of identity and justice in the adventures of part 2 display Pyle's virtuosity and control in integrating his traditional ballad sources. The same control is manifested in part 3, which celebrates the fisticuffs and juvenile high jinks that make this a quintessential "boy's book." In part 3 Pyle combines his three source-ballads into a cumulative tale in which Robin and Little John collect three new recruits while undergoing three adventures threaded by a common theme—the advisability of choosing duty over pleasure. Pyle announces this theme in a headpiece illustration (79) reminiscent of the famous emblem depicting Hercules deciding between the stern, armor-clad lady representing duty and the soft, languorous lady of desire. In the headpiece Little John, sent by Robin on an errand to Ancaster, stands on a road diverging to that town on the left and the Blue Boar Inn on the right. The road to duty is depicted as rocky, curving, and swept by rain; the road to the "humming ale" and "sweet companions" at the Blue Boar is sunlit and straight. For Little John's choice of pleasure at the inn "he paid a great score," we are told, just as "we are all apt to do in the same case" (82). Delayed a day because of his roistering, Little John gets a cudgeling from Arthur a Bland, the Tanner of Blyth. Robin, seeking his dallying lieutenant, gleefully witnesses Little John's drubbing and, after accepting Arthur into the band, moralizes to a bruised Little John about the wages of choosing pleasure over duty. In the original ballad (Ritson 2, ballad 6), to which this theme is alien, Robin, not Little John, engages with the tanner in a bloody battle. Pyle's extensive changes of the original ballad enable him to emphasize his theme and to avoid depicting Robin's defeat.

Robin is, however, soon after defeated by his own nephew, Will Scarlet, whose appearance alone deceives Robin into thinking him a Norman fop. After Will joins the band, the tanner sings an Arthurian ballad, "The Wooing of Sir Keith," in which that knight embraces his duty when none else will and volunteers to help the loathsome lady who comes to court begging to be healed by the kiss of a virginal knight. At his kiss, the lady is transformed into a beautiful damsel who offers Sir Keith her hand and fortune. Thus, Pyle adroitly returns at the end of this second adventure to the theme that unifies part 3: "a duty which seemeth to us sometimes ugly and harsh," explains Will Scarlet, "when we do kiss it fairly upon the mouth, so to speak, is no such foul thing after all" (104).

The concluding adventure offers a final variation on the theme with Robin, Little John, Arthur, and Will being thrashed by Midge the miller's son because they forget their duty toward "an honest craftsman" (even though Midge repeatedly reminds them of it) and prefer their pleasure in pretending to rob rather than protect him. Feigning that his gold is hidden in his sack of flour, Midge tricks the tricksters by throwing handfuls of flour into their faces and cudgeling them. When Robin is at last able to cough out his name, Midge retorts that "Stout Robin never robbed an honest tradesman" (110), emphasizing that even a joking deviation from duty can carry painful consequences. This conflict between duty and desire was to become one of the central unifying themes in Pyle's later Arthuriad.

Parts 4 and 5 portray Robin offering disinterested aid to those in need, a duty enjoined on him by the code to which he has bound himself. Set at the center of the work, these episodes emphasize Robin's compassion for "those that walk in sorrow" (161), apparently for Pyle Robin's most admirable trait. In part 4 Robin forges domestic harmony out of discord by restoring to the grieving minstrel, Allan a Dale, his true love Ellen, bartered by her franklin father to the rich old Norman, Sir Stephen of Trent. This conflict between the franklin's greed and Robin's notions of romantic love anticipates a Swedenborgian preoccupation with love explored more fully in the later folktales. Inspired by an Arthurian ballad detailing the pure love of Sir Caradoc, Robin offers to help Allan without the personal enrichment demanded by the Robin of the original ballad (Ritson 2, ballad 8). Before he can engineer the marriage of Allan and Ellen, however, Robin must find a priest not in league with the knight, a plot contrivance that allows Pyle to splice into this tale the ballad of Robin and the Curtal Friar (Ritson 2, ballad 10). The introduction of Friar Tuck talking and singing animatedly to himself as he devours a huge meat pasty affords one of the most engaging passages in the work, and the final confrontation between Robin and the two High Churchmen, both luxuriously dressed and prone to unpriestly ribaldry about women, explains the great animus the Bishop of Hereford and the proud Prior of Emmet hold against Robin in subsequent adventures. Part 4 concludes with the fairy-tale triumph of love over cupidity celebrated at a merry nuptial feast in Sherwood, to which, laments the narrator, "you and I were not bidden, and pity it is that we were not" (154).

In part 5 the compassionate Robin moves from the domestic to the social arena to succor Sir Richard of the Lea, a knight soon to be dispossessed of his estate by the avaricious Prior of Emmet. "Invited" to dine in Sherwood, Sir Richard has nothing to pay his host because "by ins and outs and crookedness of laws" he has been forced to borrow money from the implacable prior against his lands to bail out his son who has accidentally killed a knight. On their arrival in camp Robin discovers that Little John has by chance "invited" the Bishop of Hereford and his attendants to Sherwood. After making his guests comfortable, attending himself to their needs, Robin asks Hereford, "the richest Bishop in all England" (167), to have compassion on Sir Richard and help him meet his unjust debt. On the bishop's refusal, Robin takes a third of the bishop's rich store for his own coffers and another third for charity before lavishing on Sir Richard gold enough to pay his debt as well as costly fabrics, gold spurs and chain from his own treasury, and twenty of his men as temporary retainers.

The second half of part 5 is an inversion of the first. Robin's hospitality in the greenwood is contrasted to the inhospitable prior's refusal to lift Sir Richard, who kneels on the hard stones of the refectory floor during the whole of their colloquy. Robin's liberality is reversed by the prior's failure to offer the knight even a goblet of wine. And Robin's charity and generosity are countered by the prior's refusal to pardon or extend Sir Richard's debt. The irony inherent in this tale is clear: Rob-

in is more lawful than the man of law or the sheriff present as sup-
porters at the prior's table, more charitable than the prior whose
religion elevates charity to a cardinal virtue. Robin is the just man who
is a fugitive from justice, the outlaw who upholds the spirit of the law.
He serves in parts 4 and 5 as a moral and legal touchstone to reveal
the avariciousness and greed so prevalent in the world beyond the borders of Sherwood.

In part 6 Pyle further portrays the outlaw as ironic moral center in
a world that protects the rich and powerful in their depredations
against the poor and defenseless. Robin Hood's legendary fame derives
in large part from his stealing from the rich to give to the poor. In a
series of cleverly narrated episodes integrated from the ballad tradition
(Ritson 2, ballads 14, 19), Pyle explores Robin Hood's role as redis-
tributor of wealth and arbiter of social and economic justice. In the
adventures of part 6 Robin and Little John encounter two hypocritical
priests who "wring hard-earned farthings out of the grips of poor lean
peasants" (194), four sturdy beggars who turn out to be "thieving
knaves" (209), and a corrupt corn engrosser who manipulates grain
prices so as to induce famine and thus extort great sums "from the
needs of poor people" (210). In disguises appropriate to the Franciscan
ideal they here espouse, Robin dresses himself as a beggar and Little
John as a strolling friar to relieve these villains of those ill-gotten gains
that, according to Robin, "will be better used for charity and the good
of my merry band than in the enriching of such knaves as these" (209).
Thus money originally stolen from the needy is in turn retrieved by
the dispossessed for charitable redistribution to the poor.

Robin Hood's famous extralegal altruism explains that double perspective from which he and his band are characteristically viewed
throughout the book. As Robin himself tells Sir Richard in part 5,
"one man calleth me kind, another calleth me cruel; this one calleth
me good, honest fellow, and that one vile thief" (160). This double
perspective characterizes the way Robin is viewed by his king and
queen as well. Earlier, in part 1, Henry II had dismissed the sheriff's
request for aid in capturing Robin because he saw the bandit as merely
a petty regional thief. By part 7 Robin has assumed national promi-
nence, reigning over Sherwood "like an independent sovereign," as
Ritson put it.[12] Summoned to London under her protection by an admiring Queen Eleanor to shoot against the king's best archers, Robin
effortlessly triumphs, suggesting to the furious king that not only does
Robin vie with him for sovereignty in Sherwood but his martial prow-

ess outstrips the king's own. When the king reneges on his promise to grant Robin forty days' safe conduct and sends after him a thousand men, Robin is forced, after a harrowing chase and many close calls, to return to London to beg the protection of the queen before he is able to retire safely to Sherwood. Thus in part 7, a conflation of two ballads with variations and additions (Ritson 2, ballads 12, 13), Pyle not only explores the dual perspective from which Robin is viewed but also demonstrates that Robin's increasing fame is accompanied by increasing vulnerability, that his growing power and sovereignty in Nottingham and the midcountry have earned him more dangerous and implacable foes.

These foes are at their most desperate in part 8, which chronicles "the sharpest adventure that ever befell Robin Hood" (256). Foiled repeatedly, the sheriff and the Bishop of Hereford plot to have Robin assassinated by the sinister man-beast, Guy of Gisborne, who goes about clad in a horse's hide, dressed with hair, mane, and tail outermost. With the intrusion of this monster into Sherwood, Robin's secure sanctuary is for the first time violated. Admitting that he would kill his own brother for 100 pounds, Guy declares his moral as well as physical depravity, leading Robin to engage him in "the fiercest fight that ever Sherwood saw" (260). Easily justifying this second slaying as a humanitarian act, Robin dons Guy's bloody horsehide for reasons made no clearer in Pyle's version than in the original ballad (Ritson 1, ballad 4), a ballad of extraordinary brutality in which Guy's head is cut off, mutilated so that even his mother would not recognize him, and stuck on the end of Robin's longbow. Pyle tempers this extreme violence not only in his narrative but also in his powerful illustration of the prone body of Guy viewed from the back so that its mortal wounds remain concealed (254). Disguised as Gisborne, Robin then saves Little John from the sheriff. In part 7 and the first half of part 8, then, Pyle prepares his readers for the inevitable end of Robin's free reign in the Land of Fancy. The extremity of these latest hazards for Robin and Little John suggests the dissolution of the insulating boundaries of Arcadia and the ominous closing in of Robin's foes.

This suggestion is resolved in the second half of part 8, which begins with the ironic assurance that the great changes occurring in the outer world—the accession of Richard I after the death of Henry—"did not reach to Sherwood's shades, for there Robin Hood and his men dwelt as merrily as they had ever done . . . for it was little the outside striving of the world troubled them" (256). Only two months after Guy of

Gisborne's repulsed intrusion, however, another arrival in the green-wood signals the end of Robin's carefree Arcadian life. While on a progress to Nottingham, Richard discovers the extent of Robin's power and, vowing to "clear the forest of him and his band" (273), gains access to Sherwood by disguising himself as a friar, thus adopting Robin's own role-playing to get at him. When Robin misses his mark for the first time in the archery match held to amuse his "guests," Robin refuses to accept the customary buffet from any of his men, declaring "I am king here, and no subject may raise hand against the king" (278). Full sovereignty over Sherwood is soon restored to Richard, however, after Robin agrees to receive his buffet from the "friar," just as a king may be reprimanded, not by his subjects, but by the pope. When Richard knocks Robin down and reveals himself, Robin affirms his loyalty, and he and his men are pardoned on condition that they enter the king's service.

With this bittersweet pardon, Robin grows up, enters historical time again while the pastoral Arcadia dims and fades to the melancholy strains of Allan a Dale's mysterious "doleful ditty." Though Robin's subsequent adventures in the king's service immerse him in the great world outside Sherwood and earn him the title earl of Huntingdon, they are glossed over in a paragraph as if, being the stuff of "fact" and not of "fancy," they are of little interest to the narrator or his auditors.

After beginning the epilogue with the offer to let go the hand of those unwilling to witness "the breaking up of things" (289), the narrator tells of Robin's long-delayed return to the greenwood in passages made poignant by our awareness that Robin's efforts to rebuild the lost Arcadia will be futile, that the "joys and pleasures that are dead and gone can never be set upon their feet to walk again" (289). Robin cannot return to Sherwood because he has forgotten how to live there; he cannot grow young and innocent again. In throwing off the courtly title conferred on him in the historical world, he cannot similarly throw off the habits acquired there. Thus, instead of avoiding blood-shed and direct confrontation with his enemies wherever possible, the strategy responsible for his long survival in the halcyon early days, Robin makes the fatal error of engaging with the force commissioned by King John to root him out of Sherwood. Though victorious, Robin loses all, for he soon recognizes that his old impatience and martial pride, operative in his early killing of the forester and aggravated by his late service in Richard's wars, causes the deaths of "scores of good fellows" on both sides. Robin's grief at this failure to adjust again to the world he no longer belongs to brings on the fever that his cousin, the Prioress of Kirklees, uses as a pretext to bleed him to death in hopes of official reward. Thus, in the epilogue Robin is presented as a tragic hero whose undoing by treachery is occasioned by his own fatal error. It is to Pyle's credit that he does not spare his youthful readers this dark insight. Robin's refusal to exact vengeance on the nuns and his moving death in the arms of Little John are handled with skill and restraint, making this lyrical, resonant epilogue one of the most beautiful passages in all of Pyle's prose work.

   The illustrations.   Pyle's prose artistry in *The Merry Adventures* is as rich and packed "as an egg is of meat," from prologue to epilogue studded with metaphor and with the clever aphorisms of "Gaffer Swanthold." Luxuriant word pictures are used to set mood, to suggest the passage of time in the frame binding the episodes, and to immerse the reader more fully in the "Land of Fancy." The passage introducing part 6, for example, establishes a temporal connection with the preceding adventure at the same time that it explains the restlessness Robin and his men feel after the enforced idleness of winter. An artist's eye for shape, color, and closely observed detail helps Pyle to create the scene with a clarity characteristic of the word pictures throughout:

Cold winter had passed and spring had come. No leafy thickness had yet clad the woodlands, but the budding leaves hung like a tender mist about the trees. In the open country the meadow lands lay a sheeny green, the cornfields a dark velvety color, for they were thick and soft with the growing blades. The plough-boy shouted in the sun, and in the purple new-turned furrows flocks of birds hunted for fat worms. All the broad moist earth smiled in the warm light, and each little green hill clapped its hands for joy. (187)

   This rich prose finds its visual equivalent in the abundant detail offered in the illustrations. In the frontispiece depicting Tuck carrying Robin across the stream, for example, every fold in the friar's gown, every twig on the budding thicket in the upper left, every leaf of willow and blade of cattail forming part of an internal frame at right is minutely articulated, the incremental accumulation of detail providing a texture in the picture plane as rich—but economical—as the densely textured prose of the adventures themselves. In this appropriate frontispiece a grinning Robin and Tuck look out from the Land of Fancy through a heavy border to invite the reader to join them on their merry adventures. Pyle's bold, deliberate line suggests that nothing in the illustration has been left to chance. As carefully composed as the episode it depicts is carefully plotted, this illustration, like all the others, is architectural rather than organic, linear rather than curved, though the angular lines of the central panel are countered by the graceful curvilinear flourish of the decorated floral border.

The same angular architecture characterizes the prologue illustration of Little John triumphant over Robin at the log bridge. The inner panel, again rich in minute detailing, depicts a world of action and motion: Robin rises, spluttering, from his dunking; the grasses and trees sway in the breeze; the turning blades of the mill in the background tense and flex against the force of the wind. The admirable composition of the center panel features a balance of horizontal and vertical lines. The horizontal lines of the defeated, half-submerged Robin Hood and the log bridge on which Little John stands are opposed by the dominant vertical of Little John's body echoed in the verticality of the staff, trees, posts, and windmill blades. The border contrasts with this linear composition in its curves of scroll and band encircling the iris sheath, with the dragonfly an appropriate emblem for framing the marshy setting of the inner panel.

Pyle's sense of design, evident throughout, is especially strong in the illustration depicting Robin on the verge of being captured by the king's men in part 7 (241). The wattled enclosure in the background surrounds and seems to trap Robin while the stave fence at right foreground cuts off his escape in that direction. Encumbered by quiver, bow, sword, dagger, and horn, Robin's body is snared between his longbow and its string and bound by quiver and hat straps as well as by the jerkin thongs banded across his chest. Further, the massive, ornate borders at top and bottom burden the inner panel with an oppressive weight. The composition enables the viewer to share in a visceral way Robin's own feeling of entrapment, of being hedged round by danger. This illustration typifies the overall success of Pyle's pictorial compositions in complementing the literal text so as to create those subtle impressions necessary for the full indwelling of story in reader.

In each of the ten parts of the work the full-page cuts interact with decorative borders and smaller-scaled illustrations to create interdependent design units, each containing a headpiece that sets the scene or introduces the main theme, an illuminated initial letter featuring a central emblem for the section, and a tailpiece that telescopes and summarizes the adventures recounted in the part just concluded. The epilogue, for example, features a full-page illustration depicting the dying

"Stout Robin hath a narrow escape"
The Merry Adventures of Robin Hood, 241

EPILOGUE.

Telling how Robin Hood came back again to Sherwood Forest, and how Sir William Dale was sent against him to take him. Likewise it is told how Robin Hood died by the treachery of his cousin, the Prioress of the Nunnery of Kirklees.

AND now, dear friend, — you who have journeyed with me in all these merry doings, — I will not bid you follow me further, but will drop your hand here with a "good den," if you wish it ; for that which cometh hereafter speaks of the breaking up of things, and shows how joys and pleasures that are dead and gone can never be set upon their feet to walk again. I will not dwell upon the matter over long, but will tell as speedily as may be of how that stout fellow, Robin Hood, died as he had lived, not at court as Earl of Huntingdon, but with bow in hand, his heart in the greenwood, and he himself a right yeoman.

King Richard died upon the battlefield, in such a way as properly became a lion-hearted king, as you yourself, no doubt, know ; so, after a time, the Earl of Huntingdon — or Robin Hood, as we will still call him as of old — finding nothing for his doing abroad, came back to merry England again.

"Robin shooteth his Last Shaft" and epilogue headpiece
The Merry Adventures of Robin Hood, 288–89

Robin, cradled in the arms of a grieving Little John, preparing to shoot his last shaft into the reddening west as Azrael, the angel who parts soul from body at death, waits brooding, sword in hand, in the border. Contrasting with the prologue cut where an upright Little John crows over the defeated Robin prone in the stream, here the original vertical of Little John's body crumples in grief to conform to the horizontal of the dying Robin. The following headpiece complements this focal illustration by introducing the central theme of the "breaking up of things" with the deaths of Richard, Robin, the sheriff, and the "scores of good fellows" slain in the final battle. Bordered with a band of emblematic poppies, the headpiece depicts the moon in eclipse and Death in the dark reaping among the flowers. Behind Death, however, is a bay of laurel, the promise of enduring fame with which the epilogue ends. The illuminated initial letter predicts the epilogue's catastrophic battle through its depiction of Robin shooting at his foes, a man slain with an arrow lying at his feet at lower right. Finally, the tailpiece, like those for other parts of the book, emblematically summarizes the epilogue by depicting two of Robin's yeomen mourning his loss, their heads in their hands to create a border around the final word "Finis." As in this epilogue, so each of the preceding parts of the book features its own unified set of complementary illustrations that work with the prose text to reinforce both theme and plot.

Thus picture and prose collaborate in *The Merry Adventures* to produce a classic retelling of one of the most enduring of our cultural legends. Even after a century, Pyle's *Robin Hood* still engages the modern reader—young and old—through its innocent humor, nobility, pathos, and bittersweet nostalgia for a pastoral Arcadia where nature and preindustrial man were once so closely allied that Robin and his band could blend, through the color of their apparel, into the forest that sustained them. To this day, Robin and his merry men find sanctuary in that greenwood in the Land of Fancy, eager to entertain the youthful reader sophisticated enough to negotiate Pyle's richly textured prose and to appreciate his carefully structured pictorial compositions and book design.

The Arthuriad (1903–10)

By the end of the nineteenth century King Arthur had accomplished his fabled return from Avalon, extending the conquest of his ancient British kingdom to the New World as well, and becoming a dominant myth in fin-de-siècle Anglo-American culture.[13] Mark Twain's crusade against the rebirth of chivalry in *A Connecticut Yankee in King Arthur's Court* did little to counter the influence of Sir Walter Scott, Kenelm Digby, Alfred Tennyson, Matthew Arnold, G. F. Watts, D. G. Rossetti, William Morris, Edward Burne-Jones, and others in reestablishing Arthur's reign over the literate as well as the popular imagination. "Boy culture" was especially permeated with Arthurian ideals of chivalry and courtesy, as is evidenced by the various boys' organizations that flourished at the turn of the century, most notably William Byron Forbush's "The Knights of King Arthur," a direct forerunner of Sir Robert Baden-Powell's more enduring Boy Scout movement, itself heavily embued with Arthurian idealism. Founded in 1893 by a Congregational minister from Vermont, "The Knights of King Arthur" attempted a revival of "chivalry, courtesy, deference to womanhood, recognition of the *noblesse oblige,* and Christian daring."[14] Its members, led by "adult Merlins," met at "Round Tables," adopted the names of knights for use in the outings they transformed into Arthurian quests and jousts, and were exhorted to read the numerous bowdlerized Arthuriads prepared for them by writers hoping to capitalize on the literary success of Tennyson's *Idylls of the King.*

Aware of this apparently unappeasable late nineteenth-century appetite for Arthurian works and hoping to duplicate the success of his *Robin Hood*, which had been liberally salted with Arthurian ballads and references, Pyle suggested to Scribner's in 1902 that he write "a book somewhat matching the *Robin Hood* but giving the adventures of King Arthur and his Knights."[15] Scribner's, with at least three Arthurian books already on its trade list and undoubtedly aware of the numerous versions then available from other houses, nevertheless accepted the proposal. Pyle's four-volume Arthuriad appeared between 1903 and 1910. In accepting his proposal, Scribner's had hoped that Pyle might give "a distinction both of form and of substance to the Arthur legend which would detach it decidedly from all other books dealing with the same subject."[16] In this they were not to be disappointed. Pyle's Arthuriad differs markedly from other Arthurian works for boys published around the same time, most notably Sidney Lanier's *The Boy's King Arthur* (1880), later to be illustrated by N. C. Wyeth; Mary Macleod's *The Book of King Arthur and His Noble Knights* (1900); and Uriel W. Cutler's *Stories of King Arthur and His Knights* (1904), recommended by Baden-Powell for reading by his Boy Scouts.[17] Like other such versions, these three are simple redactions of Malory, bowdlerized retellings of the *Morte* echoing the Malorian style and faithful, by and large, to Malory's basic plot. Pyle's version, however, draws from a large number of Arthurian sources, what he called "the most universally accepted narratives," and not just from Malory. Though Pyle followed "the thread of the better-known legends" because he did not think it advisable to draw upon those less well known, his work is nevertheless the product of a myriad of influences, including the Welsh Mabinogion, the various Gawaine narratives, *Ogier le Danois*, the French and German prose romances, the works of Robert de Boron, Tennyson's *Idylls*, and, of course, Malory's *Morte*.[18] Following the same impulse that guided Tennyson in the construction of the *Idylls*, Pyle added to the Malorian plot incidents of his own invention as well as adventures garnered from his extensive reading in the then-available Arthurian texts. From these sources he shaped and adapted an Arthuriad unique among the welter of simple Malorian redactions.

That Pyle's Arthuriad was as much an imaginative as a derivative work accounts for his refusal simply to echo the Malorian style retained by Cutler, Lanier, and Macleod. So tied to Malory were these redactors that they often reproduced, nearly word for word, large parts of Malory's text. For example, the passage from Malory wherein Arthur pulls the sword from the stone appears almost unchanged in Lanier and Macleod, though both regularized spelling and Macleod modernized diction.[19] Pyle, on the other hand, abandoned the powerful simplicity of the Malorian style, striving, as he himself put it, for "the same direct and homely English of the *Robin Hood* but with a more mature and poetic finish."[20] The remarkably homogeneous style of Pyle's four volumes is however, neither "direct" nor "homely"; instead, it is "enhanced"—highly adorned, detailed, and diffuse, forged of lengthy, balanced sentences, stately prose cadences, and frequent use of archaic diction. Thus for example, the seventy-eight words of Malory's lean account of Arthur's proof of kingship swell into a passage three times as long (240 words).[21] Far from feeling it necessary to streamline Malory for youthful readers as did most redactors, Pyle provided greatly elaborated settings, motives, and reactions to the incidents presented so starkly in Malory. Though occasionally degenerating into the stilted and uninspired, Pyle's complex and elaborated poetic style is appropriate to the leisurely and lingering pace at which he unfolds what he felt to be the most exalted of all narratives next to the Bible.

Like the Bible, late nineteenth- and early twentieth-century Arthuriads were intended to provide their boy readers with a code of moral conduct and with standards for manly living while on quest through the world, a central moral purpose Pyle certainly shared with the contemporary redactors. Even in the writing of his *Robin Hood* Pyle was aware of the didactic purpose to which the story of Arthur could be put: "It doth make a man better," says Robin, "to hear of those noble men that lived so long ago. When one doth list to such tales, his soul doth say, 'Put by thy poor little likings and seek to do likewise'" (116). In the foreword to volume 1 of the Arthuriad, Pyle explicitly points to Arthur and his knights as such models "of courage and humility that anyone might do exceedingly well to follow after their manner of behavior in such measure as he is able to do" (v). To emphasize what he saw as the moral instructiveness of the tales, Pyle begins and ends each episode in his first volume with an explicit didactic interpretation and injunction. Though the didacticism grows more indirect in succeeding volumes, that central moral purpose informs the whole.

This desire to instruct and delight led Pyle to adopt principles of selection and inclusion similar to those used by Lanier, Macleod, and Cutler, who bowdlerized the Arthurian story, protecting their boy readers from the incest, adultery, murder, and gratuitous violence so prevalent in the history, and removing, as Cutler put it, whatever in Malory was "so crude in taste and morals as to seem unworthy of the really high-minded author of five hundred years ago."[22] Pyle, like Cutler, felt morally estranged from much that he found in his sources: "Unfortunately," he wrote in a letter to Edith Dean Weir, "the stories of chivalry seem to be very full not only of meanness and of treachery, but of murder and many other and nameless wickednesses that discolor the very noblest of the characters—such, even, as the character of King Arthur himself." Pyle's principle of selection, then, was informed by the same wish that governed other authors of contemporary Arthuriads, the desire to represent "all that is noble and high and great, and to omit, if it is possible, all that is cruel and mean and treacherous."[23]

Such an intention places Pyle squarely in what Mark Girouard calls "the moralist tradition" of nineteenth-century Arthurian popularizers epitomized by Tennyson. On the other hand, Pyle's work exhibits an almost equal fascination with the enchantresses and femmes fatales who figure so prominently in the paintings and poems of those like D. G. Rossetti, Burne-Jones, and Morris who are grouped by Girouard into the "romantic tradition" of Arthurian popularizers.[24] Pyle's Arthurian realm is a near-Manichean world manipulated in large part by the evil enchantress Vivien, whose radiance of red and gold is countered by the quiet emerald-and-opal beauty of the good guardian Nymue, the Lady of the Lake. Though securely in the "moralist" camp with Tennyson and the Malorian redactors for boys because he always champions the right, sealing the defeat of the wicked with an explicit moral tag, Pyle nevertheless shares the "romanticist's" intense fascination with the beguiling mask of beauty so often worn by fatal and evil women in the works of Rossetti and his followers.

The place of Pyle's Arthuriad in the welter of fin de siècle Malorian retellings for boys is thus a unique one. Though allied with his competitors in didactic moral purpose and in basic principles of editorial selection, Pyle differs from them in his use of a variety of Arthurian sources, in his leisurely and elaborate unfolding of the history, in his complex, poetic style, in his fascination with magic and the workings of evil, and especially in his pen-and-ink illustrations, which function coequally with the text. N. C. Wyeth thought these illustrations among Pyle's "most important contributions to the world of art."[25]

Though Pyle's Arthuriad was an overall critical and economic success, its appearance did not evoke the nearly unanimous approval accorded the earlier *Robin Hood*, some critics complaining about the style and length of the four volumes as well as their lack of what Charles Abbott called "the compelling power" and the "warmth and fire" of some of Pyle's earlier works.[26] Surprisingly, however, one of the most glowing commendations of the Arthuriad came from that implacable foe of the medieval revival, Mark Twain, who had condemned Arthurianism in *Life on the Mississippi* as "the sillinesses and emptinesses, sham grandeurs, sham gauds, and sham chivalries of a brainless and worthless long-vanished society."[27] The Arthurian tales "were never so finely told in prose before," wrote Twain to Pyle; "And then the pictures—one can never tire of examining them and studying them. Long ago you made the best Robin Hood that was ever written and your Morte d'Arthur is going to be another masterpiece. It was a great idea. I am glad that it was born to you."[28]

The Story of King Arthur and His Knights (1903)

Like Malory, Pyle tells of the birth, reign, and death of Arthur with the accompanying rise, flowering, and fall of the Round Table. Within this overall chronological progression, however, seemingly separate tales, like islands in a stream, interrupt the historical unfolding to provide an in-depth depiction of a particular period in the chronology of Camelot. The initial volume, for example, is divided into two parts, the first chronicling the birth, accession, and marriage of Arthur and the establishment of the Round Table, and the second retarding this historical progression to provide the adventures of three worthies attracted to Arthur's court at that heady point in the reign when the Round Table has just been initiated. The illustrations, too, help to interweave these impressions of stasis and progression. The portraits, for instance, liberally scattered throughout the work, are inert and static: arrested in moments of revery or contemplation, Arthur and Guinevere, Nymue and Vivien stare steadfastly out from their icons to confront the reader directly. Countering the stasis of these placid, timeless portraits, however, are the frequent depictions of action or event, often minutely detailed so as to capture the immediacy of their subjects in ongoing time. Pyle's illustrations thus work closely with the text in volume 1, as well as in subsequent volumes, to create the impression of an alternating timelessness and progression-in-time in the chronicle.

The first volume of the Arthuriad, the most overtly didactic of the quartet, begins with "The Book of King Arthur," in which Arthur is presented for youthful emulation as the perfect knight, flawless in humility, kindness, and nobility. Like Christ, whose early history his resembles, Arthur is the lodestar, the crown, the exemplar, "the most honorable, gentle Knight who ever lived in all the world" (v). Merlin, Pellias, and Gawaine, whose exploits are revealed in the following "Book of Three Worthies," all take Arthur as their looking glass and see themselves therein as weaker men who succumb to passion and temptation. Though their stories provide cautionary examples of human frailty, they end by ennobling themselves in spite of their failures. As such, the three worthies serve in the volume to balance Arthur's ideal life with the lives most of Pyle's youthful readers may more nearly expect to live in the world—lives constrained by weaknesses to be overcome.

Pyle begins "The Book of Arthur" with a prologue providing the legend of Arthur's birth and setting the scene for his manifestation as king, omitting, of course, Uther's coveting of the married Igraine, Arthur's mother. This prologue depicts the disorder that characterizes the interregnum after Uther's death, "the dolorous land" groaning with "the trouble that lay upon it," and suggests the usual connection between Arthur and Christ, both of whom are to initiate an era "of order and peace where is now disorder and war" (3). Accordingly, the prologue ends with "the entire world . . . wending its way to London Town" at Christmas, the inns all full with those who expect the manifestation of a new king, one Merlin intimates will arise from among "those who are unknown" (5).

The following *enfances* of the hero—the winning of kinghood, of a sword, and of a wife—are familiar to any reader of Malory. In the section devoted to the winning of kinghood Pyle seems particularly interested in suggesting a corollary between Arthur's elevation to kingship and the ascent of a youth to full manhood. He especially applauds the virtues the adolescent Arthur manifests during this rite of passage: his humility and his reverence and gratitude to Sir Ector, the father whom he has now surpassed. Lest interest in the narrative supersede a grasping of the didactic intention behind it, Pyle concludes with an explicit for his youthful readers on the threshold of maturity, admonishing them to "draw forth the sword of success out of the iron of circumstance" (5) if they would be like Arthur.

Not yet the *roi fainéant* or inactive monarch weighed down by responsibility he must inevitably become, Arthur next wins his sword and consolidates his power through his personal bravery and his desire for reconciliation with the lesser kings he has overcome. The penchant for magic and mystery, so prevalent throughout Pyle's Arthuriad, is given full reign in this segment: Arthur's guardian Nymue, the Lady

of the Lake, leads him to Excalibur and even Guinevere appears as
"some tall straight angel who had descended from one of the Lordly
Courts of Paradise" (61) to heal him with an elixir when he is wounded
in battle. The segment concludes with another didactic coda wherein
Pyle compares Excalibur and its magical scabbard to Truth sheathed in
Faith and prays that his readers, too, will gird themselves with a spiritual Excalibur so as to fight the battles of life successfully. Though
these allegorical interpretations and injunctions are intrusive, their
tone is so genial and so generous that they do not offend, avoiding as
they do any hint of authorial self-righteousness.

Claiming that the whole story of Arthur's wooing and marriage has
never yet been told, Pyle next invents a fairy-tale addition to the traditional episode in order to introduce the two persistent themes unifying the entire Arthuriad—that reality is often masked by deceptive
appearances and that duty must ever curb wayward desire. In Pyle's
addition, Arthur, resembling Robin Hood in his boyish enthusiasm,
enjoys a good jest while accomplishing his wooing and affirming his
dominance over rebel princes. Informed that King Leodegrance, Guinevere's father, is besieged by a rebel king, Arthur himself goes to Ca-
meliard magically disguised by Merlin as a gardener's boy. Guinevere,
perceptive as well as virtuous, soon comes to recognize Arthur's nobility beneath his mean appearance. After defeating the rebel king's
champion, Arthur in unmarked armor overthrows Gawaine, Ewaine,
Pellias, and Geraint, whom he sends to serve Guinevere for seven days.
When they subsequently refuse one of her requests, Arthur instructs
them in knightly duty by having Guinevere command them to serve
her "gardener's boy" at table. After this lesson in humility and duty is
learned (at the cost of an unresolved antagonism between Gawaine and
Guinevere that henceforth mars their relations), the rebel king is van-
quished, leaving Arthur to marry and to establish the Round Table,
Guinevere's dowry. The episode ends with the Knights of the Round
Table vowing allegiance both to Arthur, who has earned their fealty
and proven himself fit to rule them, and to the code he lives by.

This code, however, as the second half of the volume shows, is a
difficult one for men with human weaknesses—like Merlin, Pellias,
and Gawaine—to uphold consistently. The first of the tales collected
in "The Book of Three Worthies," clearly a cautionary tale, concerns
the enchantment of Merlin and, like the myth of Pandora, serves to
explain the intrusion of evil in the earthly Paradise envisioned by Arthur. The first great enemy of the realm is Arthur's proud half sister

Morgana, who conspires with her protégée Vivien to bring about the eclipse of Merlin, Arthur's protector. Merlin's folly transforms his wisdom into his own destruction when his desire for Vivien overrides his duty to Arthur. He himself teaches the spell of his undoing to Vivien, whose cruelty and malice are ever masked by her physical beauty. The basic story is a sad and familiar one to any reader of Malory or Tennyson, but Pyle has embedded it in the larger tale of Morgana's treachery, from which Arthur is saved only through the turning of evil upon itself and through the renewed—and redeeming—loyalty of Merlin, whose last thought is not for himself but for the welfare of Arthur.

The story of Morgana's treachery is a nightmare in which nothing is as it seems: Morgana's penitence is a sham, her gift of the strong black courser brings Arthur to the waste land, the ship she launches to succor him lands him in a dark prison, the sword Excalibur she sends him is a counterfeit, the knight she beguiles to fight and very nearly kill him is his own beloved and loyal Sir Accalon. Paradoxically, Arthur is saved from Morgana's malice by Vivien, whom Pyle unconvincingly presents as not yet altogether evil, retaining "some small pity for Merlin and some small reverence for King Arthur" (177). However, a more convincing motive for Vivien's intervention, one given credibility by her later desire to kill Morgana in cold blood, lies in Vivien's pride: with Merlin dispatched, she can brook no necromantic rivals, even weaker and defeated ones like Morgana. When Arthur vows to forgive his sister "again and again and yet again if she sin against me" (201) and rebukes Vivien in front of others for her cruelty in desiring the death of her former patron, Vivien turns on Arthur with a hatred more virulent than Morgana's ever was. She appears repeatedly throughout the Arthuriad to bedevil Arthur and his knights, countered only by Nymue, the beneficent Lady of the Lake.

That mere mortal men are so much at the mercy of potent magical forces, both evil and good, manipulating the world from behind the scenes, intensifies the nightmare quality of Arthur's adventure with Morgana. Even Merlin's culpability is diminished, immediately ensnared as he is by the enchantment of the seemingly innocent magical ring offered him by a fifteen-year-old Vivien. The vision is essentially a bleak one, the implications of which Pyle may not himself have been fully aware. Making Arthur, Merlin, and Accalon so much the victims of controlling forces more powerful than they seems to deny them too large a measure of free will. And yet, without free will, how are Pyle's readers to guard themselves, as they are enjoined, "not only against sin," but also against the "folly and weakness" displayed by Merlin (152)?

The next tale, that of Sir Pellias, raises similar questions, for the central characters—Pellias, Ettard, and Gawaine—likewise seem pawns in the control of the fey Nymue who gives Pellias an enchanted necklace with the power of making the wearer beloved by all who look upon him. The irresistible force of this necklace, its enchantment "beyond the power of any man to withstand" (238), leads the central characters to break their vows and abandon their duty. When Pellias lends the necklace to his beloved Ettard, for example, she grows to despise him while his love for her increases to the extent that he forgets his knightliness and willingly brings dishonor and shame on himself and on Arthur's Round Table. Made aware of Pellias's plight by the Lady of the Lake, Gawaine goes to intercede with Ettard and falls under her spell because of the necklace, betraying his friend, failing in his duty, and even contemplating setting up with Ettard a court to rival Camelot. After curing Pellias of the fatal wound inflicted by Gawaine, Nymue marries him, thereby achieving the end for which she has plotted all along in giving Pellias the necklace. Thus Pellias, Ettard, and Gawaine are led irresistibly by a determining power stronger than they are into shame and dishonor. Could they have resisted the power of the enchantment and acted virtuously under the circumstances? Apparently not, but perhaps Pyle, since he offers the story for the "edification" of the reader (203), merely means to suggest that in the real world, desire, which often comes upon one with all the irresistible power of an enchantment, must nevertheless be curbed lest it lead to the dishonor into which Pellias and Gawaine fall.

The story of Sir Gawaine that follows begins with an episode that again redounds to Gawaine's discredit in his refusal of mercy to a defeated knight and in his subsequent striking of the knight's wife who shields her husband against Gawaine's intemperate blow. This episode, instigated by Vivien's malicious gift that transforms the amity of two brothers into bitter enmity, ends with Guinevere's scornful accusation that Gawaine has broken his vow of knighthood.

The second episode, devoted to Gawaine's rehabilitation, is informed by Pyle's persistent theme of the necessity to subjugate desire to duty. An expansion of "The Ballad of Sir Keith" earlier included in *Robin Hood*, this episode splices together motifs lifted from "Sir Gawaine and the Green Knight" and "The Wedding of Sir Gawaine and Dame Ragnell."[29] After Arthur strikes off the head of a knight-enchanter without harm to him, the enchanter offers Arthur a reprieve if he can return within a year with a solution to the riddle, "What is it that a woman desires most of all in the world?" (300). Arthur is given the answer by an ugly hag—"That which a woman most desires is to have her will"—upon his promise that she may marry the knight of the Round Table she most fancies. She chooses Gawaine, whose great love and faithfulness to Arthur lead him to acquiesce without demur. After Gawaine passes this redeeming test of his knighthood, the loathly lady appears before him radiantly beautiful, and, on granting her her will as to whether she shall be beautiful by day and ugly by night or the reverse, she rewards him with beauty by day as well as by night. To conclude the episode, Pyle's narrator draws a lengthy allegorical significance: that just as the hag appeared ugly to Gawaine, "so doth a man's duty sometimes appear to him to be ugly and exceedingly ill-favored unto his desires." When, however, that man weds himself to his duty, "then doth that duty become of a sudden very beautiful unto him and unto others" (311). Nowhere else is this theme, a resonating chord throughout Pyle's Arthuriad, given such explicit pronouncement.

The illustrations.   Much of the success of *The Story of King Arthur and His Knights* stems from the wonderful Düreresque pen drawings complementing the text. Pitz thought these illustrations, done toward the end of Pyle's career, had "greater depth and power and a richer execution" than even the illustrations for *Robin Hood*.[30] For the Arthurian pictures, Pyle eliminated the heavy decorative borders setting off Robin Hood's Land of Fancy from the everyday world. Perhaps because Pyle intended that his readers take the Round Table knights as models of behavior and Arthurian chivalry as a code on which to pattern life in the real world, the Arthurian pictures, unmediated by any barriers except for simple line frames, invite easy access to Arthur's realm. Thus, a calculated immediacy, absent from the *Robin Hood* illustrations, characterizes both the Arthurian portraits and the action pictures that distill from Pyle's elaborated text the essence of character and event. On the first page of volume 1, for example, the reader is invited into Arthur's realm by a frontispiece portrait of the king, a telescoped encapsulization of his character and function. Standing against a blank white space, Arthur sets the globe held in his left hand against a backdrop vision of castle and gardens glimpsed through a casement, the implication being that Arthur will, at least for a time, transform the realm he rules into a civil and fruitful place. That Arthur

ing Arthur of Britain.

"King Arthur of Britain"
The Story of King Arthur and His Knights, frontispiece

is the way into this regenerate realm is implied by his extended left arm, the line of which initiates the path leading through the garden to the castle. Contrasting with the following portrait of the stern Uther Pendragon, overlord of a rude and violent realm, the portrait of Arthur closely resembles the depiction of Christ in nineteenth-century religious paintings, most notably Holman Hunt's *The Light of the World*. With admirable economy, then, Pyle employs the initial portraits of the volume to contrast the reign of Arthur with that of his father and to summarize the essence of Arthur's nature and actions.

Guinevere's portrait (78), too, is a richly suggestive icon, a distillation of her character and the events she precipitates in the narrative. Her portrait is studded with emblems suggesting both the harmony she brings to the realm with her dowry of the Round Table and the strife she introduces at the narrative's conclusion. The harmonious balanced effect of placing the central figure between two trees is emphasized by Guinevere's thick braids and by the two gentle hills that rise on either side of her. This balance, however, is offset by the two knights who strive against each other in the distance at Guinevere's left, a typological emblem suggesting both the youthful Arthur's early duel in the winning of his queen and those fatal final clashes over her that end Arthur's reign. This temporal telescoping of early hope and later disaster is echoed in the darkened sky and castle in the background, connoting both the promise of dawn and the finality of sunset, a cosmic cue used again only in the later portrait of Galahad, that apotheosis of purity and nobility who brings Arthur's reign its greatest glory on the eve of its collapse. The effect of interwoven harmony and strife in the portrait is emblematized in the sweet but thorny Renaissance rose Guinevere holds gingerly between thumb and forefinger. Her portrait, then, provides a complex distillation of Guinevere's character and the initial and final roles she plays in the Arthurian history.

The portraits of the Lady of the Lake (150) and of Vivien (162) also indicate the essential natures of these two magical women, the one a bountiful guardian figure and the other a femme fatale responsible for so much of the mischief besetting Arthur's realm. The portrait of the Lady of the Lake captures her otherworldly serenity and beauty through the interplay of vertical and horizontal lines. The trees, braids, hair ornaments, and vertical folds of garment all echo the upright frontal figure of Nymue set against the tranquil horizontal line of the lake behind her. The pellucid, quiet quality of this portrait contrasts mark-

xcalibur the Sword.

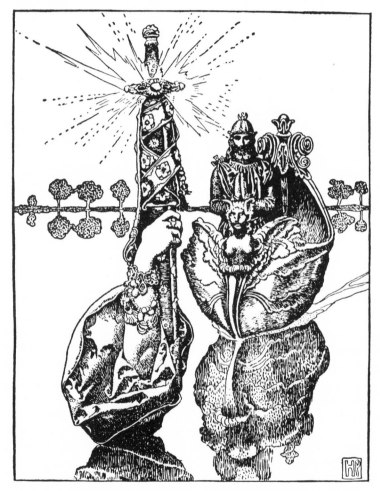

"Excalibur the Sword"
The Story of King Arthur and His Knights, 64

edly with the sinister coiling lines of the portrait of Vivien who "enmeshes" and "entangles" Merlin and weaves him in the "web" of her enchantment (177). Unlike the vertical figure of the Lady of the Lake, the central figure of Vivien is subtly serpentine in its curve of head and torso, her hair gathered in a golden net and bound by the curving line of a cobra fillet, her wand tipped with a twining adder. In the background a road twists through a clotted landscape to a castle at Vivien's left.

In addition to these static iconic portraits, Pyle also included illustrations meant to draw the reader into the event depicted. Though, in a letter to Henry Cabot Lodge, he had complained that the illustrator's art "is not capable of so much movement and vivacity" as the writer's, he nevertheless strained against the limitations of the two-dimensional visual medium in an attempt to immerse the viewer in a visceral way in the event depicted.[31] In "Sir Kay Breaketh His Sword" (8) Pyle forces his viewers to participate in the violence of the joust. The illustration is a spiky swirl of tunic, helmet plumes, dust, mane, tail, and skirt of horse. The spear-shaped horse's ears and the spiked outlines of armorial griffins echo the sharp points of sword, shields, and elbows. The whole, an extreme closeup, surrounds the viewer in the violence and turmoil of the duel. Another method of drawing the viewer into the event through a depiction is Pyle's frequent use of a depth perspective that seems to invite the viewer into the plane of the picture. In "Four Knights Serve the Gardener Lad" (112), for example, the viewer stands just behind the seated Arthur and stares out with him at the menacing faces of the knights. Similarly, in "The White Champion" (100) the viewer is placed directly behind Arthur to confront with him Gawaine and Ewaine as they advance down the road. This compositional device is used again in "Excalibur the Sword" (64) where the viewer is located by the arm proffering the sword and is thus able to watch Arthur gliding reverently up to receive the emblem of his power. This foregrounding of the viewer, who is thus given a participatory vantage point in the event, again occurs in "Queen Morgana Loses Excalibur His Sheath" (190) and in "Sir Gawaine Sups with Lady Ettard" (254) and is a most effective means of involving the reader-viewer directly in the event depicted.

This fine interplay of richly evocative illustrations with a text fully detailing sights, scents, textures, and sounds accounts in large part for the seeming authenticity of Pyle's highly artificial romantic world and for his success in making his readers at home there.

The Story of the Champions of the Round Table (1905)

The second volume of Pyle's Arthuriad introduces Launcelot, Tristram, and Percival, whose adventures constitute the flowering of Arthur's reign. Though all three knights have to do with magical ladies and prove their knighthood in similar ways, they differ in their essential roles in Pyle's scheme for the volume. Launcelot is the excellent knight-errant, the exemplar of altruistic service, the disposer of "ill-custom" in the world. He is the standard against whom all other knights are to be measured. Tristram, on the other hand, is the paragon of earthly love and fidelity, the steadfast knight in the face of overwhelming trial. He is the good knight in the real world, hated for his virtues by wicked men. The concluding story of Percival amalgamates features from each of the preceding tales. Like Launcelot, Percival is a puissant knight devoted to altruistic service, though he is not as wedded to the human world as Launcelot is whose youth was spent with Nymue in her enchanted lake. Like Tristram, too, Percival engages in an unhappy love affair, though he sublimates his earthly love into a more potent spiritual one. The story of Percival thus offers variations on the themes introduced in the first two segments of the volume and completes the careful plot symmetry characteristic of all of Pyle's works.

Launcelot's *enfances*, like Arthur's in the preceding volume, provide a model for youth soon to enter the adult world and dedicate themselves to its betterment. Sending Launcelot forth, the Lady of the Lake endows him with a ring to dispel enchantment and counsels him to prove himself through actions, not words—"for it is better," she says, "for the world to proclaim the worthiness of a man than that the man should proclaim his own worthiness."[32] Once he has moved from magical childhood to adulthood, from Nymue's enchanted Castle of the Lake to Arthur's kingdom, Launcelot is filled with love for the flawed human realm and vows "to make this world in which I now live the better and the happier for my dwelling in it" (59). Filled with a missionary zeal, Launcelot embarks on a series of adventures involving a tidying up of his world, the ending of all "ill custom," the freeing of prisoners unjustly held, and the restoration of the weak to rights denied them by the wicked. After proving his prowess against the enemies of the Round Table, Launcelot concludes his *enfances* by posing in jest as Sir Kay to overthrow Ector, Gawaine, Ewaine, and Sagramore, thereby establishing himself as the greatest of all Arthur's knights. That the reader is to identify with Launcelot Pyle leaves no doubt, exhorting his audience to "take example of the noble Sir Launcelot" who proved himself "at all times worthy in the performance of his duty" without "the hope of reward, or of praise" (84). Since Launcelot's legendary adultery with Guinevere would pose a serious obstacle to his being so taken as a model for youth, Pyle denies that any adultery ever took place: "Now I am aware," he states, "that there have been many scandalous things said" concerning Launcelot's relations with Guinevere, "but I do not choose to believe any such evil sayings" (23). Avoiding Pyle's direct approach, Lanier, Macleod, Cutler, and other Malorian redactors adopted the less happy expedient of ignoring the issue completely, leaving the reader mystified at the cause for the later animosity against Guinevere and Launcelot in Arthur's court.

Unlike the story of Sir Launcelot, the adventures of Sir Tristram are relatively free of overt moralizing, being recounted instead for the pleasure of the reader, as the narrator repeatedly declares. Pyle's account closely parallels Malory's in his depiction of Tristram as a faithful lover, a noble knight nearly the equal of Launcelot, and a man beset by sorrows not all of his own making. Pyle's version of Tristram's love affair with Belle Isoult, however, suffers from an uncritical reliance on the sentimental romantic conventions of nineteenth-century melodrama: the lovers voluntarily drink the love potion, knowing that they doom themselves to unrequited passion; Tristram remains ever chaste, unlike his amorous counterpart in Malory; and the lovers die together, roses springing up to intertwine over their separate tombs. Pyle also includes exaggerated tokens of Tristram's knightliness, having Tristram break his sword in honor of Launcelot after their duel to a draw and having him put himself in Sir Blamor's power rather than slay this defeated but unyielding cousin of Launcelot. Pyle is, on the other hand, at his most effective in portraying the pathos of Tristram's fate. He does not spare his readers the dark vision of a just man overwhelmed by misfortune, doomed to serve a wicked king whose villainy is magnified by Tristram's nobility and who succeeds in depriving Tristram of his love, honor, home, sanity, and eventually even his life. King Mark, the antitype of Arthur, is an even more potent evil force in the Arthurian world than Vivien, Morgana, and the other wicked sorcerers because his human jealousy and malice cannot be countered either by amulet or by virtue. In depicting Cornwall, the nightmare reversal of Arthur's Camelot, the tale of Tristram serves to establish the importance of Arthur in ordaining a realm where virtue and knightliness may flourish.

With the concluding story of Percival, much of it taken from the tale of Peredur in the Mabinogion,[33] Pyle again returns to the didactic

injunctions so frequently employed as explicits in the earlier story of
Launcelot, the reader being encouraged, for example, "to live as brave
and honorable and pure a life" as Percival did (259). Percival's *enfances*
are unified by Pyle's concern with the deceptiveness of appearances.
Raised in extreme isolation like Launcelot, Percival mistakes knights
for angels, rides forth in armor made of woven willow branches, con-
fuses a hamlet with "the great world," and enters the pavilion of Yvette
the Fair thinking it a church. Beneath Percival's naive antics and rustic
accoutrements, however, Yvette detects his nobility and worth, though
Sir Kay fails to see beyond Percival's rude appearance and is punished
for it. The remainder of the tale is given over to variations on the
"ending of ill custom" and "proof-of-knighthood" adventures rehearsed
earlier in Launcelot's story, though Percival's later encounter with Vivien, who changes into stones those fooled by her lovely semblance,
marks a return to the appearance/reality theme that unifies his *enfances*.
Pyle concludes the tale with an account of Percival's love affair, which,
like Tristram's, is not brought to fruition in this world. In an eerie
scene taken from the Mabinogion, Percival contemplates the blood and
black feathers of a raven killed in the snow by a hawk and is reminded
of the fair skin, black hair, and red lips of Yvette whom he finds has
died before his return to her. At the end of his adventures Percival the
virgin knight, like Tristram the courtly lover, is given near equal rank-
ing in nobility with Launcelot, all three of whom offer "a very high
example that anyone might follow to his betterment who lives in this
world where so much that is ill needs to be amended" (329).

   The illustrations.   The illustrations for this volume, though su-
perb, are on the whole not as richly textured as those for the first
volume: the figures are often smaller; the compositions are less complex; backgrounds and settings are not as fully articulated; and there
is a greater distance between viewer and subjects. Nearly all of the
portraits of the heroes—Launcelot, Tristram, Lamorack, Percival—depict very young men, stiff and uneasy in posture, seemingly unfamiliar
with repose and resentful at having to interrupt their lives of action to
stand still for portraits. The depictions of Belle Isoult, Yvette the Fair,
and Blanchefleur, on the other hand, offer more variety in stance and
costume, though they all portray wistful Pre-Raphaelite women who
seem to contemplate their sorrows. Almost all of these portraits feature
a distant castle in the background, visual equivalents of the many prose
passages throughout the text describing vistas in which these castles
are first beheld as the various knights and ladies approach them.

he Lady Yvette the Fair.

"The Lady Yvette the Fair"
The Story of the Champions of the Round Table, 268

"The Lady Yvette the Fair" (268), perhaps the best of these portraits, is another of Pyle's complex icons. It captures the short-lived Yvette as if on the verge of her departure for the next life. Marked for an early death, she stands delicate and tenuous in profile, facing westward out to sea away from her castle home in the background and holding a lily and a ring, emblems of her purity and faithfulness to Percival. Her dress is brocaded with birds seemingly poised for flight, and the sweep of her hat behind clearly suggests a raised wing, these avian images appropriate for one whose death is prefigured for Percival by a raven slain in the snow. To her right a ship glides away from land, its sails filled with the wind which blows from behind her.

Many of the action pictures interspersed with these portraits show the same depth from foreground to background used repeatedly to organize the illustrations in the preceding volume and to draw the reader into Arthur's world. For example, Nymue, bearing the infant Launcelot away from his mother into the lake, walks toward the viewer (2). Similarly, Launcelot, recounting his adventures to Hilaire and Croisette, is thrust into the foreground of the picture plane where we may hear his tale too, his other auditors depicted in the background (54). Finally, when Tristram beats King Mark with the flat of his sword, the king runs towards the viewer, Tristram following in middle ground and Isoult cowering in fear behind them both (220).

Though, taken as a whole, the illustrations from the first volume are more successful, many of these action pictures are as beautifully conceived as any of their predecessors. The picture of the Queen of Ireland attempting to stab Tristram in the bath, for example, is a vigorous swirl of hair and draperies with Tristram flinching under the baleful arch made by the two men wrestling with the enraged queen (132). In the picture of Lamorack herding Nabon's swine Lamorack's stance is almost exactly echoed in the blasted tree at left, a forceful and economical image suggesting the mental and physical affliction the captive Lamorack suffers (208). Certainly one of the most successful of these pictures is that of Mark spying on Tristram. Sprawled across a spare background of rigorous verticals—the wall, the drapes, and the glaive pole—is the S-shaped figure of Mark. A bright band of light from the room occupied by Tristram and Isoult shoots through the opened arras into the shadows where Mark lurks contemplating murder as the climax of his malice (252). As with those of the first volume, these illustrations collaborate with the text to vivify the adventures of the heroes plotted for the entertainment and edification of the reader.

The Story of Sir Launcelot and His Companions (1907)

The third volume of the Arthuriad concerns the further adventures of Launcelot, his marriage to Elaine (a surprise for readers familiar with Malory), and the birth of Galahad. Interspersed with these events are the stories of Gareth and Ewaine, though these seemingly intrusive tales are absorbed into the fabric of the volume through the variations they offer on the dual themes of the deceptiveness of appearances and the necessity of performing one's duty even when contrary to desire. The tales in this volume, then, all mesh in a carefully structured thematic unity.

The story opens with the abduction of Guinevere and her May-court by Sir Mellegrans. After his horse is killed by Mellegrans's archers as he comes to Guinevere's rescue, Launcelot sacrifices his pride and embraces his duty in spite of his repugnance at having to ride in the fagotmaker's cart like a criminal bound for execution. Applauded by Guinevere, whose correct vision allows her to see Launcelot's sacrifice and the consequent nobility of his deed, Launcelot is nevertheless so severely rebuked by his kinsmen blind to all but appearances that he exiles himself from the court for two years and adopts the sobriquet "Le Chevalier Malfait" ("The Knight Who Hath Trespast"). Thus Pyle cleverly adapts this tale, traditionally involving Launcelot's defense of Guinevere against charges of adultery, into an appropriate introduction to the two interwoven thematic dialectics—appearance versus reality and duty versus desire—upon which all of the tales in the volume are structured.

Interrupting the subsequent adventures of the self-exiled Launcelot is the tale of Sir Gareth, the archetypal "Bel Inconnu" or "Fair Unknown." Gareth refuses to go to Camelot in royal array because he prefers to win acceptance and honor for his deeds rather than for mere external accidents of dress and lineage. In spite of his yeoman green, many of the noblest knights, including his uncle Arthur and brother Gawaine, recognize Gareth's nobility beneath his humble appearance, though Kay and others scorn him as a mere kitchen knave. When the Round Table knights refuse to perform their knightly duty in helping a lady in distress because Lynette will not reveal her besieged sister's name or degree, Gareth volunteers, apparently unconcerned with such externals when his duty is clear. Lynette, however, exhibits the same blindness as the knights she reprimands because she continues to scorn Gareth for what he appears to be, obstinately failing to recognize the valor of his deeds as he overcomes knight after knight. Her sister Lay-onesse, on the other hand, looks beyond what she thinks is Gareth's low station and accepts the deed that proves his faithfulness to knightly duty. Because of this, she is in the end rewarded with a knight noble in station as well as in action.

Following the tale of Sir Gareth, Pyle returns to Launcelot's adventures to explore with convincing psychological accuracy the intense conflict in Launcelot between duty and desire. Nursed by Elaine after being wounded in a tournament, Launcelot falls in love with her, and Pyle makes it clear that Launcelot's duty at this point involves entering into a mature adult relationship rather than continuing his platonic but nevertheless dangerous attachment to Guinevere. Launcelot, however, is divided between his duty to Elaine, for whose happiness he knows himself responsible, and his desire to return to the old feckless adolescent camaraderie at Camelot where, unburdened with the responsibilities of marriage and stewardship, he may lead again the boyish life of action so similar to the life led by Robin Hood's merry men. Pyle insists, however, that Launcelot's earlier vow of knighthood to the queen in no way precludes a commitment to Elaine, especially because Guinevere already has the love and service of the worthiest knight of the realm. When the tormented Launcelot returns to Guinevere, claiming "I have left all my duty and all my service and all my hope of peace and happiness and have come to thee," she spurns him, driving him insane.[34] Launcelot endures this penalty for his deviation from duty for several years until he wanders back to Corbin and is cured by Elaine. Their marriage and life together at Joyous Isle are marred, however, by Launcelot's continuing conflict: "Down, proud spirit, and think not of these things, but of duty," Launcelot repeats to himself when tempted to abandon Elaine for the pleasures of the court (197).

At this point of tension in the plot Pyle interrupts Launcelot's conflict to tell of Ewaine and the Lady of the Fountain, a tale from the Mabinogion restructured to serve as a corollary to the Launcelot story. After winning the love of Lesolie and pledging to guard the enchanted fountain, Ewaine, like Launcelot, yearns to escape the bonds of mature duty for the carefree days of his adolescence spent in Arthur's court. When Lesolie encourages him to take a short respite from his duty, Ewaine meets Vivien on his journey to Camelot; she gives him a ring of forgetfulness. After Ewaine has been carousing at Camelot for some time, Lesolie's sister appears at court to accuse him of unfaithfulness to his vow, whereupon he sets forth at Arthur's bidding to discover the cause of this reprimand. Having forgotten his duty, he is stripped of his armor (and thus of his knighthood) by a gang of thieves who, fortunately, also steal the ring. Thereafter, disguised as a pilgrim to expiate his sin, he is reconciled with Lesolie, marries her, and thereafter remains steadfast.

Launcelot and Elaine, however, are denied this happy ending because Launcelot once again abandons his duty to Elaine and capitulates to his desire for Guinevere. Persuaded at last to return to Camelot, Launcelot and Elaine face together the jealous wrath of the queen, who eventually finds a pretext to banish Elaine from court, but only after Elaine has overheard her tell Launcelot that his duty and faith mean little if they work toward their unhappiness. When Elaine rides forth sick and alone to a priory, her brother Lavaine accuses Launcelot of being "dishonored as a knight" and a traitor to his troth for leaving "his own lady for the smiles of another woman" (307).

Ending this episode with the assurance that "God was even then preparing a great punishment" for the unwitting Launcelot, one from which "he might never hope to escape for as long as he should live" (308), Pyle turns in the concluding section to the nativity of Galahad. This section opens with an entertaining diversion in which Gawaine, seeking to destroy Vivien, is transformed into a misshapen dwarf and serves as a lady's pet, protesting vainly that "I am not what I appear to be" (317). Nymue brings to a close the volume's last excursion into the appearance/reality theme by restoring Gawaine to his normal shape, but not before Gawaine hears Merlin prophesy from a mist about the coming of Galahad and the quest for the Grail. Pyle then turns to the culmination of the Launcelot story: Elaine dies after giving birth to Galahad and her funeral barge floats down the river to Camelot, a stunning reproach to Launcelot for his desertion. The volume concludes with the hermit's moving admonitions to the despairing Launcelot concerning the mercy of God to sinful man.

The economical identification of Elaine, the daughter of King Pelles, with Elaine, the Fair Maid of Astolat, is only one of the many liberties Pyle took with his sources in composing this work, the most unified and least derivative volume in his Arthuriad. The traditional Arthurian tales from Malory and the Mabinogion are reworked and interwoven into a carefully patterned tapestry of repeated themes and motifs. In addition to its thematic cohesiveness, the volume is further unified by its focus on Launcelot. Even in the stories of Gareth and Ewaine, apparent digressions from the main plot, Launcelot plays a significant role, knighting Gareth and initiating Ewaine's quest. Finally, unlike most Malorian redactors for boys, Pyle succeeds in humanizing Launcelot by disclosing the weaknesses that color his nobility. Launcelot is Pyle's most completely delineated character in the Arthuriad—and his most endearing and sympathetic.

Unlike the first two volumes, the success of this work stems primarily from the text, the illustrations being, for the most part, less innovative, almost perfunctory. Though there are the familiar portraits of wistful women and stiff young knights, even the best of these portraits—those of Layonnesse (76) and of Elaine (frontispiece)—do not serve to distill character in the complex and economical way that the icons of Guinevere and Yvette do in the preceding volumes. The portrait of Elaine, for example, depicts a maiden simple, innocent, and good, but one perhaps too robust to be withered by Launcelot's neglect. The illustrations portraying actions and events are characterized by a certain sketchiness and lack of compositional inventiveness, with the exception, perhaps, of the concluding "Barge of the Dead" depicting the corpse of Elaine laid beneath a sail emblazoned with a queen (the triumphant Guinevere?) sitting in state beside a crown and heraldic shield (334). The figures depicted are often smaller and thus must be viewed from a greater distance against their thinly textured backgrounds. Though Pyle still provides many of these illustrations with that depth arrangement that invites the viewer into the scene, the invitation seems somehow less cordially extended. This apparent decline in the quality of the illustrations coincides with the growth of Pyle's interest in mural painting and his antipathy for grinding out the medieval magazine illustrations then so much in demand.

The Story of the Grail and the Passing of Arthur (1910)

Before concluding the adventures of Arthur, Pyle cautions his readers that "all endings are sad, and the passing of any hero is a sad thing to tell of."[35] Unlike Tennyson in the *Idylls*, however, Pyle does not emphasize the tragedy of Arthur's final defeat. Instead, he prefaces his final volume with the story of Geraint, who achieves his greatest glory while in apparent decline, a fitting preamble to the subsequent account of the Grail quest, an achieved conjunction of the human and the divine and thus the culmination of Arthur's reign. The tragic concluding story is then tempered by Pyle's optimistic certainty that Arthur's eclipse is only a temporary one and that the glory of his return will soon revivify a world darkened by his disappearance.

The Mabinogion story of Geraint and Enid with which the volume begins belongs thematically to the group of tales collected in the preceding volume. Plot incidents involve success or failure in detecting the true nature of characters and events and the performance or neglect of duty. Geraint, for example, perceives Enid's nobility beneath her impoverished appearance, but later, in the gaiety of life at Arthur's court, he fails to detect her complete fidelity to him. So dispirited is he by his suspicions that he takes her to his estate, where he sinks into lassitude, neglecting his knightly duties. In the long trial they undergo together, Enid, though mistreated, proves her faithfulness beyond doubt and Geraint takes up again his duties as knight. Pyle apparently separated this tale from those with similar themes and used it to initiate the history of the end of Arthur's reign because it tells of a knight past his prime who is forced out of a too-early retirement to prove his prowess once again. Just as Geraint undergoes his greatest test and achievement in his maturity, so Arthur achieves his final and greatest glory in the Grail Quest just before his realm sinks again into darkness.

Pyle plumbs the Grail Quest for its rich didactic value, arranging the adventures of Launcelot, Percival, Bors, and Galahad according to their instructive value for adolescents. Galahad, for example, whose *enfances* recall Arthur's in his acquisition of a sword, must triumph over two brothers, representing "Pride" and "Cruelty," as well as ten knights, representing the "ten deadly sins," before he can achieve the Grail. As with Spenser's knight, Galahad's allegorical adventures are signed by the red cross he wears as emblem. His father, Launcelot, is prevented from attaining the Grail by his old sin against Elaine. So it is, concludes Pyle, "that the sins that one hath committed follow one through one's life and in the end bring the soul such distress and failure as that which Sir Launcelot here suffered and endured" (107). Percival, on the other hand, achieves the Grail after his purity is successfully tested against the sensual wiles of the enchantress Vivien, and Bors, too, succeeds after foregoing the pleasures of marriage, wealth, and worldly power in his steadfastness to duty. In a farewell admonition concerning this dominant theme in his Arthuriad, Pyle concludes that "duty lyeth before all the pleasures and all the glories of the world, wherefore he who doeth his duty under all circumstances . . . cannot go astray in his performances" (127). Thus Pyle uses the Grail Quest to catalog those virtues needed by one who would achieve the highest success in life—strength, sincere repentance, purity, and devotion to duty. This is the summary and culmination of the moral lessons scattered so liberally throughout the preceding volumes.

The passing of Arthur after the glorious achievement of the Grail follows the familiar history as recorded in Malory, except, of course, that Pyle denies Launcelot's adultery with Guinevere, attributing Arthur's fall instead to fate helped along by the malice and contentiousness of certain of the Orkneys. Arthur does not die, but is taken to the Arcadian isle of Avalon by Morgana and the Lady of the Lake, the enmity between these two enchantresses apparently resolved. This culmination of Arthur's history is prepared for in the volume's illustrations as well as in the text. Though these final cuts share the sketchiness and thin texture of those in the preceding volume, Pyle invests many of them with a sense of foreboding and gathering gloom. The darkened sky backgrounding the frontispiece portrait of Galahad, for example, suggests that same dawn/dusk ambiguity used so effectively in the first-volume portrait of Guinevere: Galahad's arrival signals the dawning of Arthur's highest glory at the same time that it portends his decline and the sunset of his realm. No such ambiguity operates in the dour portrait of Mordred (222), glowering out from under hooded eyes against a black sky luridly illuminated by the moon over the sea at Dover. Mordred, the final destroyer of Arthurian chivalry, stands on the rim of the abyss and is denied the ubiquitous chivalric castle backgrounding almost all of the other portraits in the Arthuriad.

More subtle than these culminating portraits, however, is the depiction of Arthur negotiating with the bishop for an end to the war with Launcelot (184). Pointedly echoing the initial volume's frontispiece depicting a youthful Arthur directing the orb in his left hand into the paradisal garden seen through the casement, this illustration depicts a tired king now with his back to that garden, his left hand devoid of the orb, his left arm bent away from the casement and no longer guiding us through it, his head resting wearily on his right hand now empty of his scepter. Thus, in these two illustrations, Pyle succinctly rounds the wheel of fortune from the bright, joyous young king just beginning his reign in the first volume to that king's collapse into grief at the end of his reign. Altogether, Pyle's numerous Arthurian illustrations spaced between these two depictions are an impressive pictorial achievement.

In concluding his Arthuriad, Pyle joins those who believe that the time for Arthur's millennial return "is now nigh at hand," for, Pyle argues, "less and less is there war within the world, and more and more is there peace and concord and good will amongst men" (246). The optimism with which Pyle bids farewell to his readers in 1910 is, of course, stunningly ironic, given that Arthur's ancient kingdom would be harried a scant four years later by an apocalyptic world war. Certain cultural historians, including Mark Girouard, have suggested that Britain and America entered this disastrous war equipped with a naive and dangerous enthusiasm engendered at least partially by a nine-teenth-century cultural idealization of Arthurian chivalry fostered by the numerous adaptations of Malory made available for youthful emu-lation. Pyle, however, was to be spared this irony by his death in 1911. With almost uncanny presentiment he begins and ends this last volume with thanks to God for sparing him for the seven years required to conclude his Arthuriad and with a prayer that he might live yet longer in order to achieve other works as well. But it was not to be. *The Merry Adventures of Robin Hood* and the four-volume Arthuriad, both classic adaptations of traditional materials, were to be the bookends of Pyle's literary career.

Chapter Three
Fairy Tales and After

With the publication in 1886 of his first collection of fairytales, *Pepper & Salt,* Howard Pyle established himself as the premier American envoy to fairyland, a territory explored and all but annexed as a British colony by such eminent Victorian fugitives from the Industrial Revolution as Dickens, Ruskin, Thackeray, Charles Kingsley, George MacDonald, Oscar Wilde, Andrew Lang, and Joseph Jacobs. Closely allied with his British counterparts in producing "literary" as opposed to "traditional" or "folk" fairy tales, Pyle impresses his narratives with a dominant authorial personality—playful, witty, colloquial, and at times deftly didactic. Unlike traditional folktales wherein plot incidents often appear arbitrary or haphazard due to unclear character motivation or lapses in causal sequence, Pyle's literary fairy tales feature coherent elaborations of setting, motive, plot, and underlying theme. In spite of these literary embellishments, however, Pyle invariably respects traditional folktale conventions, never parodying the formulas, never condescending or "covertly sniggering, with an eye on the other grown-ups present," a manner of relating folktales condemned by J. R. R. Tolkien as the "deadliest of all."[1] Instead, Pyle presents the folktale world objectively and forthrightly, if nostalgically, often with whimsical humor but without a hint of mockery or superiority. As such, he allies himself with the Brothers Grimm (*German Popular Stories,* English translation 1823) and with the naiveté of the German peasant storytellers rather than with the arch, sophisticated, and often satirical eighteenth-century French courtly raconteurs like Perrault and his royal counterparts, the Countess D'Aulnoy and Madame le Prince de Beaumont (their collections introduced into England in the early eighteenth century).

Pyle's predilection for the Germanic folktale style over that of the French conte stems from his early exposure to various German collections introduced into the nursery by his mother, with whom he continued to share this mutual delight well into early manhood. In a long letter to her dated 26 November 1876, for example, he describes himself as having tumbled into fairyland through his reading of Thorpe's

Northern Mythology, there finding himself "turned loose in a boundless wilderness of quaint dwarfs, ugly trolls, ridiculous kaboutermanne-kens, and lively elves."[2] He was to spend roughly the next twenty years describing the wonders of this "boundless wilderness," initially in several short apprentice works for *St. Nicholas* and then for the audience of *Harper's Young People,* almost all of the many fairy tales first appearing there being later collected into three volumes, each unique in style and tone. The first collection, *Pepper & Salt* (1886), offers charming tales of homely peasant wit and shrewdness, while the second, *The Wonder Clock* (1888), features marvelous stories of magic and enchantment. The third volume, *Twilight Land* (1895), mingles narratives of European origin with exotic, richly textured tales set in Asia or the Middle East.

Pyle's explorations of fairyland also include a keen survey of its borders and neighboring territories. *A Modern Aladdin* (1892), for example, uses the traditional Aladdin fairy tale as a point of departure for an elaborate romance set in eighteenth-century France. A second romance, *The Price of Blood* (1899), also draws heavily on fairy-tale conventions and formulas, its plot a chiaroscuro of innocent love against a brooding backdrop of extravagant Oriental vengeance. And in *The Garden Behind the Moon* (1895) Pyle employs full fairy-tale conventions to create what he called "a true fairy tale," a sweet, sad, delicate allegorical myth exploring the significance of life and death. Thus Pyle's long tenure in the land of faerie resulted in some of the most important and successful works of his career, and the souvenirs from his sojourn there appear as fairy-tale motifs throughout his best-known works as well, the early *Robin Hood* and the final four-volume Arthuriad.

Genre rather than strict chronology determines the disposition of this chapter. Thus, a discussion of Pyle's three folktale collections precedes a discussion of the two elaborated fairy-tale romances and the allegorical myth, *The Garden Behind the Moon.*

Pepper & Salt (1886)

Pepper & Salt, Or Seasoning for Young Folk consists of eight tales and twenty-four picture-poems originally published in *Harper's Young People* from 1883 to 1885. Pyle may have derived his title from George MacDonald's *At the Back of the North Wind* (1871) where, in chapter 25, Little Diamond defends nonsense rhyming as "a very good thing." "A little of it now and then," he argues, "more of it for Baby, and not so much for grown people" is "like the pepper and salt that goes in the soup."[3] Pyle, too, saw the spirited tales and rhymes of this collection as offering "a little pinch of seasoning in this dull, heavy life of ours."[4] In the preface "a giddy-pated jester" lays aside his bauble and belled cap to speak seriously for a moment, defending "innocent jollity and mirth" as a necessary relief from "all the troubles, the labors, and the cares" of life. Challenged by such stern moralists as the "sober, wise man" who "shakes his head and goes his way" disapproving of the waste of time involved in idle games and "odd quips and jests," the narrator concedes the underlying seriousness of life but maintains that it can nevertheless be lent "a little savor now and then" as a restorative "to lift the corners of the lips in laughter that are only too often dragged down in sorrow" (viii). Accordingly, he promises to make "merry for a little while" those "good children" who have first learned their lessons and done their chores.

This defensive preface collaborates closely with the frontispiece wherein the jester sits cross-legged, entertaining a group of children resting in a grassy area bordered by the "stony Path of Life" and hedged by the furrowed field tilled by a farm laborer straining over his plough at upper left. This daisy-pied space represents the pastoral oasis, the temporary interlude, the respite from lessons and labors promised in the preface. From its charmed enclosure the depicted children, and the jester as well, will soon emerge refreshed to take up again the duties and the cares of life. For the moment, however, the standing girl pictured in the frontispiece as caring for the baby at the back of the group of seated children is told in the closing lines of the preface to "seat the baby on the grass" and thus to rest from her labors for awhile so that both might better enjoy the stories and verses presented for their amusement.

This direct verbal/visual interchange initiated in preface and frontispiece is continued in the picture-poems inserted throughout the work. In spite of Pyle's reservations concerning the quality of his verses, the one-page picture-poems never fail to charm.[5] In them Pyle accomplishes his boldest experiments in the interrelation of picture and text, exploring the many ways in which the verbal and the visual can interact. The cross-diagonal page design for "Two Opinions" (4), for example, forces the reader-viewer to regard poem and pictures with equal attention. The verse stanzas tell of a magpie who thinks a mute signpost intelligent when it does not interrupt his self-centered chatter, but changes his opinion when the signpost fails to direct him to shelter on a rainy day. The illustrations at upper left and lower right provide a pictorial interpretation of the poem—and more, for they add a visual story about preparedness not narrated in words. The magpie and signpost in the top illustration are superseded in the foreground of the lower illustration by a dripping, shivering minstrel walking alongside a friar who remains dry under a broad-brimmed hat donned at the onset of the cloudburst. Only this provident friar, anticipating all changes in circumstances, escapes the discomforts of the magpie and minstrel when the weather changes. In "Two Opinions," then, the illustrations collaborate with the poem at the same time that they function independently of it to tell a story not narrated in the text.

"A Newspaper Puff" (12), featuring a foolish gaggle of geese frightened by a wind-filled newspaper, offers a further variation on the collaboration of picture and poem. The page architecture consists of an interrelated series of linear perspectives: the poem, its form imitating the jerky rhythms of waddling geese, directs the eyes vertically up and down the page while the illustrations, capsulizing the action in three separate panels, direct the eyes from right to left as the geese pad along at the top of the page, from top to bottom in the central panel as the geese cluster to watch their gander confront the newspaper, and finally from left to right in the lower panel as the geese scatter in terror from the puffed-up daily. In short, the page is a map of complex visual directions designed to keep the eyes moving, now vertically, now horizontally.

The following picture-poem, "Three Fortunes" (13), involves the adventures of a shoemaker, tailor, and baker who set out to find the purse of gold at the end of the rainbow. The shoemaker and the tailor stop on the way to marry, but the baker continues on the road to nowhere, searching for an illusory fortune. The poem advises that it is better to seize the luck in one's path rather than "to toil for an imaginary thing." Like other illustrations in this collection, that for "Three Fortunes" coalesces in one picture plane a series of events distributed over time and space, unreeling with a near-cinematic quality. The camera pans down a continuous road to show the progressive stages in the fortunes of the three tradesmen. Countering the dictum that a painter can render only a single moment in time, Pyle's illustration is a graceful materialization of successive moments. This cinematic encapsulation of time and space is also featured in "A Verse with a Moral but No Name" (49), where the wise man of Haarlem is shown walking down the same continuous road asking his foolish question, growing

Three·Fortunes·

A merry young shoemaker,
    And a tailor, and a baker,
Went to seek their fortunes, for they had been told,
    Where a rainbow touched the ground,
    (If it only could be found,)
Was a purse that should be always full of gold.

    So they traveled day by day,
    In a jolly, jocund way
Till the shoemaker a pretty lass espied;
    When quoth he, "It seems to me,
    There can never, never be,
Better luck than this in all the world beside."

    So the others said good-bye,
    And went on, till by-and-by
They espied a shady inn beside the way;
    Where the Hostess fair, —a widow—
    In a lone seclusion hid; "Oh,
Here is luck!" the tailor said; "and here I'll stay."

    So the baker jogged along,
    All alone, with ne'er a song,
Or a jest; and nothing tempted him to stay.
    But he went from bad to worse,
    For he never found the purse,
And for all I know he's wandering to this day.

    It is better, on the whole,
    For an ordinary soul,
(So I gather from this song I've tried to sing,)
    For to take the luck that may
    Chance to fall within his way,
Than to toil for an imaginary thing.

"Three Fortunes"
Pepper & Salt, facing 13

ever thinner and more befuddled until at last, at the bottom of the page, the wind blows him away. Again, time and distance are condensed into an economic depiction unraveled by the eye's movement down the road. Such pictures cannot be taken in at a glance, passively; they must be read, unreeled from first to last as if on a projector. In *Pepper & Salt,* then, Pyle attempts to create what he was later to describe in *The Garden Behind the Moon*—a wonderful storybook with pictures that "moved just as real things move."[6]

Other picture-poems eschew this cinematic disposition for a comic-strip alternation of verse and illustration. The best of these is "Superficial Culture"(17) with its rollicking verse story of a pig's attempt to enter polite society. The page is composed of four panels, each consisting of a single stanza and its pictorial equivalent or ideograph. In the first three panels old dame, dancing master, and society lady incline toward the foppish pig; in the last the "dame of degree" discovers the oink beneath the lace and brocaded coat and declines away from the pig's amorous advances. "A Disappointment" (96), too, has this comic-strip or point-for-point hieroglyphic quality, each short verse being preceded by a drawing of maid or beau in an attitude appropriate to the lines being spoken.

Pyle's exuberant inventiveness is everywhere displayed in these picture-poems. In "Play and Earnest" (36), for example, he uses poetic form as an adjunct to picture. When the breeze frolics, light and merry in the tree branches, the verse lines skip on the page, alternating from long to short. When the breeze turns tempest, however, and demolishes the tree, the verse becomes a compact and forceful block on the page. On the other hand, "A Tale of a Tub" (69) features an utter regularity of verse form so as not to compete visually with the subtle, complex design of the pictorial panel at right, a harmony of echoing and interweaving circles, ovals, and crescents. Pyle's play with pictorial form and verse structure makes each picture-poem a game to delight the visually and verbally acute. These short diversions offer some of the most successful of Pyle's experiments with visual/verbal collaborations. They feature a triumphant sense of page design and pattern; a sophisticated use of verse rhythms and forms to imitate or mimic verse subjects; a characteristic insistence that the pictures tell their own stories as well as those set forth explicitly in the poems; and innovative cinematic and comic-strip solutions to the problems raised by having to depict a temporal/spatial narrative progression within a single picture plane.

Uncertain of the critical reception of these short pieces, Pyle turned his concern into a joke in the last picture-poem (97) where a lamb gambols to stave off four wolves enchanted by its play. When the lamb grows tired, however, and ceases its sport, the wolves devour it, leaving only the tail. "So with me," the narrator puns, "when I am done, / And the critics have begun, / All they'll leave me of my fun / 'Ll be the tale." Though the eight remaining "tales" in the collection represent some of Pyle's earliest experiments with the folktale, they already feature his storytelling trademark, a carefully modulated voice—simple, colloquial, always affable—that draws the reader into a casual, comfortable relationship with the narrator, almost as if intimate friends have come together to chat, amusing themselves with clever quips and homely metaphors drawn from a common fund of shared references, acquaintances, and anecdotes. In "How Dame Margery Twist Saw More than Was Good for Her," for example, Pyle extends a metaphor into idle, amusing gossip when he tells of the fairy husband blowing out the light in the good dame's right eye until "it was blind as the stone wall back of the mill, where Tom the tinker kissed the miller's daughter" (41), and in "Farmer Griggs's Boggart" he describes each hayrick in the winter fields as wearing a dunce cap of snow, "like the dull boy in Dame Week's school over by the green" (69).

Such metaphors are appropriate for tales united by their celebration of domestic shrewdness and peasant wit. Like the picture-poems, each tale elucidates a simple moral without being cumbersomely didactic. In the stories of Dame Margery Twist and Clever Peter, for example, Pyle demonstrates the penalties one must suffer when one fails to keep one's counsel, and in "Claus and His Wonderful Staff" and "Hans Hecklemann's Luck" he shows how greed invariably leads to disaster. A number of tales, including the initial and final ones in the volume, celebrate the advantages of domesticity and a happy marriage. In "The Skillful Huntsman" Jacob must first prove himself provident enough to marry Gretchen, who in turn proves herself a suitable and worthy wife by saving her husband through her cunning from abduction by the horse-hoofed "Red One." The narrative's coda consists of an explicit moral, that "many another man beside Jacob Boehm would find himself in a pretty scrape only for his wife" (13). "The Apple of Contentment," a Cinderella story, is also an epithalamion wherein the beautiful goose girl Christine brings contentment through marriage to the unhappy young king grown "melancholy and sick for want of that which he could not get" (103). Thus the tales of *Pepper & Salt* are primarily *Hausmärchen,* tales of unpretentious folk wisdom set for the most part in cottages and by humble hearthsides.

This homely, domestic character of the tales reflects their origins in the folk traditions of Britain and Germany, Pyle's primary sources being the folktale collections of Joseph Jacobs and the Brothers Grimm. A number of the tales in *Pepper & Salt* involve an artful cementing of motifs borrowed from various narrative sources, while others are literary elaborations of received tales. The first half of "Claus and His Wonderful Staff," for example, is lifted from the Grimms' tale of "The White Snake," wherein the hero comes to understand the speech of birds and beasts after eating a small portion of the fabulous reptile served up regularly to his wise master; and the concluding segment of "The Bird in the Linden Tree" closely parallels the ending of Jacobs's wonderful tale of "The Black Bull of Norroway" where the true bride, displaced by a false one, succeeds on the third night in revealing her identity to her prince.

More interesting, perhaps, than this borrowing of motifs is Pyle's reconstruction and adaptation of tales taken over complete from his sources. The simple tale from Jacobs of the "Fairy Ointment" becomes in *Pepper & Salt* "How Dame Margery Twist Saw More than Was Good for Her." Just as his title is six times longer than Jacobs's, so Pyle's story is similarly elaborated with detail, commentary, and multiple incident. He begins the tale with a direct moral statement absent from his source: "If one could always hold one's tongue as to what one sees, one would be the better for it" (28). He then invents the subplot involving Dame Margery's fabulous tulip garden, setting the narrative nostalgically in an idyllic age "before the smoke of the factories and the rattling of the steam-cars had driven the fairy folks away from this world into No-man's land" (29). After nursing the fairy wife, Dame Margery applies only to her left eye an ointment given her to deprive her of fairy vision, but so garrulous is she that she cannot refrain from calling out to the fairies she sees with her right eye as they gambol in her tulip bed. The fairies flee, leaving her fabulous tulips as ordinary as anyone else's, but still Dame Margery does not learn to hold her tongue, losing the sight in her right eye when she upbraids the fairy husband at the fair for "scraping good luck and full measure off of other folks' butter" (41). To Jacobs's simple tale Pyle brings added character delineation, particular descriptions, an explicit moral or theme, and invented incidents to make the narrative uniquely his own. He does the same with "Farmer Griggs's Boggart," an expanded version of Jacobs's "The Cauld Lad of Hilton."

Connected in style and tone, the tales in *Pepper & Salt* are further unified through their illustrations. Unlike the diverse illustrations provided for the picture-poems, eclectic in their borrowings from Dürer, Greenaway, Caldecott, Walter Crane, and others, the pen-and-ink drawings for the tales feature a common style, one later to be used by Pyle's student, Maxfield Parrish, whose bespectacled kings and bemused pages and peasants would appear on magazine covers, signboards, and advertisements well into the twentieth century. Like the integration of picture and poem in the short pieces in the collection, the story illustrations collaborate closely with their texts, even to the extent of Pyle's directing the reader in several stories specifically to the pictures, a feature found only in this collection. In "The Skillful Huntsman," for example, the Red One sets the magic plow before Jacob "and it grew large as you see it in the picture" (7), and in "Farmer Griggs's Boggart" the family is driven out of the cottage, "just as you see in the picture" (76). So insistent is Pyle on this collaboration of illustration and text that he appends to the illustrations elaborate banners bearing explanatory legends, and he places the pictures on the page so as to surround them with prose, only occasionally granting an entire page to an illustration.

Pyle's unfailing sense of design is at its strongest in "Farmer Griggs's Boggart" where a number of the illustrations interrelate in a continuous pictorial narrative. In the first picture, for example, Farmer Griggs smokes his pipe by his hearthside, a sleeping dog curled at his feet (70). On turning the page, one sees the other half of the hearth where Dame Mally Griggs sits spinning opposite her husband (72). With admirable economy, the following page shows Farmer Griggs standing by the open door conversing with the boggart, the cold air gusting in on Dame Mally in the preceding illustration, prompting her to insist that the irresolute Griggs shut the door after the boggart has entered (73). The following full-page cut (77), one of the most successful of all the illustrations in the collection, depicts the Griggs family moving from their cottage to escape the pest, the resigned farmer and his wife leading the procession, followed by their children on the back of the horse which pulls the cart with their belongings, the unshakable boggart perched on their butter churn at the top of the page. Such illustrations and the tales they help to tell combine with the twenty-four

Frontispiece and title page
The Wonder Clock

picture-poems to make *Pepper & Salt* a worthy successor to *Robin Hood* and one of Pyle's most delightful contributions to American children's literature.

The Wonder Clock (1888)

Venturing beyond the humble hearthsides featured in the stories of *Pepper & Salt,* Pyle ushers his readers into a realm of magic and enchantment in *The Wonder Clock,* a collection of twenty-four "marvelous tales" originally told in *Harper's Young People* from 1885 to 1887. Entry into this enchanted realm is gained through an initial series of complex visual designs. In the frontispiece an aged Father Time, his scythe and hourglass discarded at his feet, has taken on his knee and sheltered with his wings a laurel-crowned youth to whose music he listens entranced under a tree newly burst into blossom. In this depiction Pyle promises entry into a realm of story where, as Tolkien put it, we may "stand outside our own time, outside Time itself,"[7] where Time's hourglass, tipped on its side, no longer chronicles a progression toward sorrow and dissolution. The youthfulness of the wing-sheltered laureate further suggests that the tales themselves, many of ancient folk origin, have long withstood the passage of historical time to remain ever fresh, appealing anew to each generation. This implication also governs the following illustrated title page depicting a faun piping to a Golden Age gathering of animals and birds, the predators and their prey at peace, all held spellbound in a pastoral, Edenic landscape arbored with ripe grapes and shaded by a tree heavy with fruit. From a branch depends a banner bearing the legend "Ita Primo, Ita Semper" (As it was in the beginning, so it will always be). The following preface headpiece unites the two preceding illustrations through its depiction of Father Time sitting cross-legged, smoking a pipe and grinning with glee as he peruses this book of stories, his back turned to his scythe and hourglass.

In the preface the narrator gains access to this "Wonderland" through his "dream-cap" and comes to Father Time's house, "a house as old as the world itself," where he meets Time's grandmother spinning in the sun.[8] Seeking "odds and ends," apparently with which to construct his tales, the narrator is conducted to Time's garret, where he finds first "all manner of queer forgotten things which had been laid away" (v) and then the Wonder Clock itself which has not worked "since men began to grow too wise for toys and trinkets" (vi). In his rewinding of this ancient clock, Pyle allies himself with those nineteenth-century Romantics—Andersen, Dickens, MacDonald, Andrew Lang, and others—who helped to refurbish the folktale after its banishment to "Time's garret" during a rational, utilitarian age which had devalued tales of wonder as mere remnants of the childhood of the race, embarrassingly naive and fortunately outgrown. For the individual, too, Pyle rewinds the Wonder Clock, impoverished as he or she is for whom the stuff of childhood—story, wonder, enchantment—is banished by adult cares. Thus in his preface Pyle heralds the cultural rediscovery of the Wonder Clock, of that which had been hidden away and all but lost, but which after all "will never wear out, no matter how long it may stand in Time's garret" (vi).

The Wonder Clock, ticking once again, strikes the hours with "a pretty song," a reference to Pyle's sister's verses for the hours, each of which announces a dance performed by the "drollest little puppet-figures," apparently the characters in the tales. According to the narrator, however, the Wonder Clock has grown a little rusty from disuse so that the puppet figures at times "danced a dance that I knew as well as I know my bread-and-butter," and at other times "jigged a step I had never seen before," as if "a dozen or more puppet-plays had become jumbled together among the wheels back of the clock-face" (vi). So, too, some of Pyle's narratives in *The Wonder Clock* are adapted directly from well-known sources, usually from the Grimms, while others "jumble together" elements from a variety of traditional tales so as to create a tale never before told. He concludes the preface with an invitation to the reader to join him in Wonderland. The transit accomplished via the dream-caps which all own, Pyle again winds the Wonder Clock, and the book begins, the following headpiece for the table of contents depicting a jester (resembling Pyle himself) piping into Wonderland the same children, including the girl holding the baby, pictured in the frontispiece for *Pepper & Salt*.

The preface to *Pepper & Salt* had been concerned that children take refuge in Wonderland only now and then, when free from the duties of daily life. They were not to dwell there. The alternation of Katharine Pyle's verses depicting ordinary domestic life with the tales of enchantment in *The Wonder Clock* carries the same implication: the daily world of lessons and labors is the solid ground over which Wonderland is built and to which one must inevitably repair. The verses, tiny slices of life, capture a central tone and activity characteristic of the hour they toll and are accompanied by appropriate illustrations as well as astronomical and meteorological information. For example, "One O'Clock" features the old house cat prodding from room to room, "her green eyes shining through the gloom," to find all fast asleep. The verse is accompanied by an Art Nouveau flourish depicting a smiling bat centered in spiky-leaved poppies. At "Two O'Clock" a black cock crowing in the moonlight is answered by a red cock, causing the maid Gretchen to turn in bed and the hound to stretch before settling down again. At "Five O'Clock" Gretchen pokes the fire, startling the Kobold asleep on the hearth and rousing the Goodman who wakes his wife. And so the day proceeds: at "Eight O'Clock" the children go to school; at "Twelve O'Clock" (Gemini ascendant and the weather "Dry and Hot"), the men come in from the fields for a dinner of bread, soup, cabbage, and beer; and at "Nine O'Clock" Dame Margery treads through the sleeping house, listening at each door to assure herself that all is well before retiring. This safe ordinary diurnal progress through the book serves to counterbalance the world of the tales where the extraordinary becomes the ordinary. These verses thus provide safe points of departure and return for those who venture into Wonderland.

Longer, often more complex, and of greater variety than the tales in *Pepper & Salt,* the *Wonder Clock* narratives nevertheless retain the engaging, colloquial, even playful authorial voice featured in the earlier collection, though the youthful and ingratiating exuberance of *Pepper & Salt* has been restrained, and direct authorial intrusion held more in check. With this elevation in style and tone comes an elevation in subject matter, most of the tales featuring kings, princesses, and royal marriages rather than humble peasants. In the märchen, beast fables, and drolls collected in *The Wonder Clock,* Pyle enters his maturity as a storyteller, employing the conventions of the folktale naturally, flexibly, and with telling effect. He mined the folktale collections of the Brothers Grimm in a variety of ways, including direct borrowing, imitating, expanding or contracting various source tales, and jumbling together different motifs to create essentially new tales. Thus, "Mother Hildegarde" is a direct, though secular translation of the Grimms' saint's legend, "Mary's Child"; "The Step-Mother" is an imitation of "Snow White"; "Bearskin" offers a contracted version of the Grimms' lengthy "Two Brothers"; "How Two Went into Partnership" expands the Grimms' short "The Cat and the Mouse Set Up Housekeeping" and adds to it incidents from "Clever Gretel"; "How the Princess's Pride Was Broken" is a conflation of Andersen's "The Swineherd" and the Grimms' "King Thrushbeard"; and "The Simpleton and His Little Black Hen" is constructed around a clever motif lifted from the Grimms' "A Good Stroke of Business." Thus Pyle shows himself in this collection less an inventor of original tales—like MacDonald, Andersen, and Wilde—than an adaptor of traditional tales for a modern audience. He was, however, certainly more than a scholarly collector and editor of folktales like Andrew Lang and Jacobs. Though Pyle's tales are baked of the dough kneaded by many anonymous oral tellers, his renditions and adaptations are unique and engaging in style and tone, vivified by incomparable illustrations, and carefully reworked with a cleverness, a verve, and a simple clarity that make them seem fresh even to a contemporary twentieth-century audience.

Pyle seems fascinated with these stories first as narratives and then as vehicles for moral instruction. Though his didactic intention is everywhere felt in the collection, it is less obtrusive than in the tales of *Pepper & Salt,* most of which conclude with a moral tag. The growing subtlety of his instructional impulse is made clear in the conclusion to "Cousin Greylegs, Ye Great Red Fox, and Grandfather Mole" in which the "moral" is left for the reader to derive: "Now in our town we do not make puddings without plums, or tell a story without rhyme or reason, but if you wish to find any meaning in these words, you must put on your spectacles and look for it yourself, even though the tale stands all legs and no head, as the man-in-the-moon said about his grandmother's tongs" (88). The "plums in the puddings" form a compendium of values regarded highly by Pyle and his late nineteenth-century American contemporaries. The second tale in the collection, "The Water of Life," for example, cautions about the illusiveness of appearances and applauds faithfulness to duty, dual themes threading throughout the later four-volume Arthuriad. A beautifully structured tale, "The Water of Life" draws its basic situation from the Grimms' "Faithful Johannes" and weaves into it motifs from "East of the Sun, West of the Moon" and even "Cinderella." The story features a king who ruthlessly exploits a faithful servant, claiming as his own the servant's heroic deeds. A princess, wooed by the king, sees through his ruses and bestows her hand on the servant as a reward for his bravery and for his faithfulness even to a faithless master. In "How Three Went Out into the Wide World" a wily fox lures a goose, a cock, and a sausage, unwilling to supply their masters with down, wake-up calls, and stuffing, into the woods where "every one can live for himself! and nobody else" (42). The inadvisability of living selfishly is made clear when the fox eats each in turn. "Mother Hildegarde," another of these tales with a simple theme, revises the hyperdulic Grimm tale of "Mary's Child," with its Catholic theme of the forgiveness awaiting those who penitently confess their sins, into an exemplum stressing the necessity of being truthful.

But the moral most frequently propounded is that generosity insures happiness and often monetary rewards as well, while greed and avarice guarantee grief. That this theme underlies over a third of the twenty-four tales in the collection suggests the uneasiness with which Pyle and his contemporaries reacted to the American postbellum industrial boom then transforming the social, political, civic, and economic structures of the nation and creating an opulent "Gilded Age" during which the Morgans, the Vanderbilts, and their aristocratic cohorts accumulated their vast personal fortunes. Again and again in the tales, gold is associated with disaster, wealth with unhappiness, avarice with misery and death. Only those who do not overvalue riches and consequently descend into greed can be happy in their possession. Thus, "One Good Turn Deserves Another" concerns a fisher lad's acquisition of the "key to wish-house" and the great wealth it brings, but concludes happily with his demand that the princess accept him first in his rags before he will marry her. In "The White Bird," a rendition of the Grimms' "The Golden Bird," three princes seek an apple from the Tree of Happiness. Unlike his elder brothers, the youngest prince avoids luxury and excess on his journey, working to earn what he needs. Tainted with avarice, however, he fails two important tests because he believes that "if happiness is to be found in anything, it is to be found" in the gold and silver guarded so jealously by the sleeping giants, dragons, and armed men (112). His lesson learned, he later confronts a dangerous witch, her golden hair obviously emblematic, and when she offers him whatever he desires, he steadfastly demands the White Bird, a bewitched princess who reverses the eventual treachery of the prince's two brothers and restores him to his proper place as heir to the throne. At the end of the tale the fortunate prince has earned the apple of happiness, the sword of power, and, best of all, the love of the White Bird through his dutifulness and hard work and his victory over avarice and greed.

Other tales structured according to this theme are "Master Jacob," in which an avaricious priest, provost, and mayor hurl themselves into a deep pit seeking illusory gold; "The Simpleton and His Little Black Hen," in which Caspar outwits his brothers and a landlord made vulnerable by their incapacitating greed; and "How the Good Gifts Were Used by Two," in which a rich brother's cupidity is constantly foiled. However, Pyle's clearest statement of the theme appears in "Which Is Best?", a tale featuring a dialectic between a rich man, "covetous and greedy," and his poor but "kind and merciful" brother (205). The poor brother loses his nag and both of his eyes when his wagers that "mercy is better than greed" are decided against him in favor of the rich brother by a grand lord, a rich merchant, even a poor ploughman (206). His sight fortuitously restored, he uses the black pebble given him by an old woman in exchange for his alms to enter a fabulous storehouse where he bypasses an egg-sized diamond and caskets of gold and jewels to choose a leaden chest containing a book of knowledge, a pair of truth-revealing spectacles, and an apple guaranteeing relief from all sorrow and sickness. When his rich brother sees how happy his life has become, he borrows the magic pebble in spite of his brother's warning that "I have brought away all that is worth the having" (214). When the rich brother unwisely chooses the diamond, he is plunged into darkness, a metaphorical blindness in which he is doomed to wander until his death. "So," Pyle concludes in his most direct statement of this major theme in *The Wonder Clock,* "mercy and temperance were better in the long run than greed and covetousness," seeking confirmation from his sidekick Tommy Pfouce, who ends this tale with an adroit final reference to the images of sight and blindness, encouraging readers to "put on your spectacles" and look at the story "from the right side" (215).

As in *Pepper & Salt,* Pyle concludes *The Wonder Clock* with an epithalamion, having in earlier stories also praised marriage, most notably in "How One Turned His Trouble to Some Account" where a princess counsels her father, correctly as it turns out, that the personified Trouble dogging a soldier's footsteps "might leave him if he were married" (32). "The Best That Life Has to Give" closes the collection with a narrative incorporation of the key Swedenborgian tenet that "true marriage love" is emblematic of the fundamental love of heaven and earth, the spring of all other joys both here and hereafter. Pyle brings the tale to a close with an elegant compliment to his wife Anne: "And did the queen really get the best in the world? Bless your heart, my dear, wait until you are as old as I am, and have been married as long, and you will be able to answer that question without the asking" (318).

As is clear from the preface, Pyle considered his primary audience for *The Wonder Clock* to be children. Appropriately, then, he delineated in the tales what Tolkien called the second of the three faces of fairy stories, the magical face, de-emphasizing the mystical face (revealed in the adult fantasies of George MacDonald, especially *The Phantastes* and *Lilith*) and the scornful or pitying face satirizing human foibles (the face revealed in certain of Perrault's tales and in others by Ruskin, Thackeray, and Dickens).[9] Pyle was, however, aware that his tales of magic also showed to older, more sophisticated readers Tolkien's satirical face, since they chronicle the pride, the prevarications, the greediness, and the cruelties of the "droll puppet-figures" set dancing by the chiming of the Wonder Clock. Thus, on the book's end-page Pyle appends a Latin caution against cynicism, counseling his more sophisticated readers not to hold all in derision, for there is that which is human even in man's most perverse follies. The tales in this collection, like those in *Pepper & Salt,* invariably avoid cynicism, enchanting their readers by their ease, unselfconsciousness, and naiveté, the three traits that Roger Sale saw as characterizing "a good deal of the best American children's literature."[10] The tales satisfy Bruno Bettelheim's criteria for successful folk fairy tales in that they depict with essential optimism "the symbolic struggle of personality integration," intimating "that a rewarding, good life is within one's reach" if the quest for "true identity" is bravely undertaken even in the face of adversity.[11]

The illustrations. *The Wonder Clock,* however, apparently falls under that censure Bettelheim reserves for storybooks accompanied by illustrations, which he sees as directing "the child's imagination away from how he, on his own, would experience the story," thus robbing the child of those important personal meanings derived from applying "his own visual associations . . . instead of those of the illustrator."[12] What Bettelheim fails to take into account, however, is that the pictures of a great illustrator like Pyle can actually train a child to see, can shape taste, providing the ore-images from which a child can forge a richly visual imaginative life. Rather than stifling the imagination, they can liberate it. Such is the case with the illustrations for *The Wonder Clock,* among the most beautiful ever penned by Pyle. The book follows an unvaried design protocol, each story being complemented by an emblematic headpiece, an illuminated initial letter resembling an old woodblock, and four illustrations with black-letter titles providing visual equivalents for the tale's central events.

The illustrations mesh with the tales to emphasize the effects of "recovery, escape, and consolation," which, according to Tolkien, all fairy tales should provide. By "recovery" Tolkien means an estrangement from the familiar, a renewed sense of the "queerness of things that have become trite," a transformation of the tamed into the "dangerous and potent," the "free and wild."[13] Though most of the illustrations focus on the specifically human scenes in his narratives, Pyle does provide an aura of recovered mystery in his depictions of giants, dwarfs, or haloed saints, in his illustrations of thoroughly domesticated animals in the beast fables, and even in his use of various archaic styles of dress, ranging from idealized Renaissance garb to eighteenth- and nineteenth-century costume, a temporal spectrum suggesting the freedom granted a traveler in the realm of story to range over time. The first full illustration from "The Clever Student and the Master of Black Arts" (53) best captures this effect of recovery, for in it Pyle startles his viewers with a glimpse of an animistic universe where a student, disguised as a fish, can convert himself into a ruby ring and leap into a princess's basket so as to save himself from a pike, the guise of his treacherous master. Pyle depicts these extraordinary feats in a setting animated by the wind, an "ordinary" mystery which, though it cannot be seen, nevertheless flexes the blades of a windmill, fills the sails of a ship in the background, and billows the princess's clothes and hair.

This adroit juxtaposition of natural with preternatural mystery invests each with something of the other so that the ordinary world shares in the extraordinariness of the realm of story, allowing too the recovery of this world as a fitting place for the enactment of wonder.

"Escape," as Tolkien uses the term, involves not only a fleeing from poverty, sorrow, death, and the disorder and chaos of our world, but also from the ancient limitations that, since the Fall, hedge us round, preventing us, for instance, from flying or conversing with other living things.[14] This effect of "escape" fascinated Pyle, not only in the narratives but also in the illustrations, one of the most beautiful drawings in the volume being the second illustration in "The Water of Life" (21) depicting the faithful servant flying on the back of the North Wind. Every detail in this careful composition stresses the exhilaration of flight: the Wind's two huge wings arch into powerful, feathered crescents imitating and reversing the delicate curve of the quarter-moon beneath them; the servant's billowing cloak gusts out behind him to complement the garments of the North Wind whipping in his wake; and the wings of the line of geese at lower left echo the winged helmet of the servant at upper right. This fascination with escape underlies other illustrations as well, including the delicate headpiece depicting Princess Golden-Hair carried away on the wings of the great Black Raven (65), Peterkin poised with his magical goose on the back of the little gray hare as they flee the pursuing giant (183), and the swan wafting the prince away over darkened fields and towns in "The Swan Maiden" (233).

For Tolkien, however, the most significant of the effects of faerie is "consolation," the moment of "sudden and miraculous grace," the fleeting glimpse of "joy beyond the walls of the world, poignant as grief."[15] To illuminate such moments, Pyle repeatedly exercises his greatest skill, producing the most beautiful and successful illustrations in the volume, among them the princess's rescue from the dragon in "Bearskin" (9), the joyful recognition by the princess of her ragged liberator in "The White Bird" (119), and the king's deliverance of the maiden from the pit and his later recognition of her under enchantment in "The Step-Mother" (155, 159). The joyful culmination of Princess Golden-Hair's hard odyssey through the House of Death and on to the end of the earth in search of the Raven Prince is captured in a beguiling illustration of the princess, her feet bandaged and her dress in tatters, enfolded at last in the Prince's arms, her face illuminated by her heart's ease, both haloed in the arch of a luminous window (75). Finally, the

The Princess knoweth the Young King .

"The Princess knoweth the Young King"
The Wonder Clock, 277

lovely depiction in "How the Princess's Pride Was Broken" of the
king's raising the ragged princess from the depths of her humiliation
(277) provides a perfect example of that consolation resulting from
what Tolkien called the sudden, joyous "turn" following a "eucatas-
trophe," in this case the shallow, grasping princess's being cast into
miserable poverty so that she might learn to love. The illustration
derives its power in part from the virtuoso textural contrast of the
princess's coarse homespun with the king's opulent cope of sculpted
gold. In the princess's face, penitent and abject, glimmers a first faint
reflection of the tender solicitude with which her husband at last turns
to her with forgiveness. Such enchanting illustrations, fit accompaniments to the tales, help to make *The Wonder Clock* Pyle's best book of

fairy tales and his own personal favorite. Henry Pitz includes it with *Robin Hood* and *Pepper & Salt* in what he calls a "triumvirate of masterpieces."[16]

Twilight Land (1895)

Pyle clearly intended *Twilight Land* to round out a series initiated by *Pepper & Salt* and *The Wonder Clock,* the frontispiece to this third collection of fairy tales being a farewell conflation of images from the two preceding volumes. The central androgynous figure in the *Twilight Land* frontispiece, for example, wears the cap and bells of *Pepper & Salt*'s jester and the gown and wings of *The Wonder Clock*'s Father Time. In addition, the *Twilight Land* illustration is set in a flowering, fruit-laden dell similar to the one depicted on the title page of *The Wonder Clock,* except that the time is now dusk and the rapt animals of the earlier illustration are replaced in *Twilight Land* by *Pepper & Salt*'s audience of children, including the girl holding the baby. Both *The Wonder Clock* title page and the *Twilight Land* frontispiece bear the motto "Ita Primo, Ita Semper."

As in the two earlier collections, the introduction to *Twilight Land* ushers the reader into a land of fancy, "a wonderful, wonderful place" where "no wind blows the dust into your eyes or the chill into your marrow."[17] In this land, where "all is sweet and quiet and ready to go to bed" (1), the narrator drifts along the road "as a soap-bubble floats before the wind, or as a body floats in a dream" (2), past trees, bushes, a mill, past the inn with the Sign of Mother Goose, almost out into "the Land of Never-Come-Back-Again," that ominous place abutting the boundaries of Wonderland from which Pyle guarded his youthful readers in *The Wonder Clock* by repeatedly drawing them back through his sister's verses into the world of lessons and chores after their excursions into the realm of enchantment. Catching himself on a blossoming apple-bough, the narrator returns to the taproom of the inn where Mother Goose herself introduces him to the "rag-tag lot" gathered there, including Aladdin, Ali Baba, Fortunatis, Jack-the-Giant-Killer, Dr. Faustus, Bidpai, Cinderella, St. George, and other characters culled from the diverse cache of world lore, legend, and folktale. Unlike the brief prefaces to the preceding collections, which conclude before the tales begin, the introduction to *Twilight Land* extends as a frame throughout the work, each tale preceded and followed by commentary from its fictional narrator, the whole concluding on the last page of the volume when the pleasant Land of Twilight vanishes as "a breath fades away from a mirror" and the narrator opens his eyes again on "the work-a-day world" of his library where his family, "my own dear people," have gathered around the fireplace (437–38). Thus, like Chaucer, Boccaccio, and the earlier anonymous collective authors of *The Fables of Bidpai* and the *Arabian Nights,* Pyle uses a framing device to tether the *Twilight Land* tales, their diversity in theme and cultural setting reflecting the similar diversity in their individual narrators.

These chroniclers tell tales appropriate to their cultural origins and reflecting their own adventures. In other words, Pyle matches tales to tellers, inventing stories suitable in plot, theme, or incident for his fabled narrators to recite, a task made difficult by the necessity of avoiding a too close duplication of the teller's own story and yet touching on it sufficiently to suggest the similarities. In "Empty Bottles," for example, Dr. Faustus tells the tale of the student Gebhart who desires to study under Nicholas Flamel, philosopher, magician, and conjuror of demons. Gebhart vows to resign wealth, rank, and pleasure for the sake of wisdom, and Flamel seems to accept him as his pupil, offering him refreshments. The plot abruptly shifts ahead at this point to Gebhart's final test of faithfulness, a test he fails, succumbing to a princess's temptations of love and wealth. Just as Gebhart raises the dagger to dispatch his master, Flamel rouses him from what the reader at last understands to have been a trance, dismisses him as unworthy to be his pupil, and orders his servant not to bring the food after all. No better narrator could be found for such a tale than Dr. Faustus, a man possessing the knowledge and power of Flamel but beset as well with the weaknesses and base desires of Gebhart.

This appropriateness of narrator to tale also characterizes "A Piece of Good Luck," Cinderella's tale about a friend of hers and "how she looked after her husband's luck" (194). The tale concerns Jacob Stuck and the piece of good luck he uses to control a genie endowed with all the powers of Cinderella's fairy godmother—and then some. Jacob falls in love with a proud princess, arranges for her to visit him (but has her home by the stroke of midnight each time), and eventually proves himself her acceptable suitor after she initiates a search for the man to match a purloined lock of hair. The tale concludes with the princess's saving Jacob and her father from the exile imposed on them by an evil prime minister and her refusal to hand over to her husband the lucky piece he has in the end mismanaged, a nice feminist touch. In "Where to Lay the Blame," too, Pyle matches tale with teller. Patient Grizzle, herself the archetypal long-suffering wife, narrates the story of a good woman who advises her loutish fisherman husband to help an old man for the reward he offers. Losing a hatful of gold because he foolishly violates several easily obeyed proscriptions, the fisherman returns home to lay the blame for his loss on his wife.

This subtle interweaving of tale, narrator, and frame makes *Twilight Land* the most complex and carefully structured of Pyle's three folktale collections and insures a greater originality in the narratives, few of which can be traced directly to Jacobs, Grimm, or any other popular source, though they contain motifs familiar to any reader of fairy tales. Extending beyond the strictly European tales featured in the preceding collections, *Twilight Land* includes stories set in the Middle East, India, and the Orient as well as Europe. These tales often feature an elegant diptych narrative structure, sections of which are elaborated with a Wildean excess of jewels, fabrics, scents, melodies, and textures, the narrative frames seeming at times to totter beneath this freight of gorgeous and exotic detail. The majority of the *Twilight Land* tales feature spirits and demons, are far less colloquial and less overtly didactic than the simpler tales of the earlier volumes, and frequently deal with more sophisticated concerns, often depending for their resolutions on some sort of ironic turn or inversion, or ending with the failure of a foolish hero. A representative tale, Ali Baba's "Not a Pin to Choose," is set "in a country in the far East" and involves the fortunes of the fagotmaker Abdallah who finds a purse with a hundred gold pieces. Personally frugal, he nevertheless lends money to his spendthrift friend Ali, who eventually turns on him. Cautioned by a sage not to think ill of Ali since "no man loveth another who is always giving" (266), Abdallah acquires a genie who, from small to great, first feeds and clothes him, then helps him win a princess, and finally makes him Emperor of the World. That accomplished, Abdallah chafes under his debt to the genie, orders him into a casket, and sinks him into a deep well, there being at last "not a pin to choose" between the ungrateful Ali the fagotmaker and the thankless Emperor Abdallah. While this tale, with its ironic, though predictable, concluding inversion and with its unusual theme of the burden of gratitude, represents a decline in the beguiling innocence and naive charm of the earlier tales, it nevertheless demonstrates a growing sophistication in the use of the folktale form, a sophistication ultimately leading to certain of Pyle's longer adult romances, themselves variations on folktale plot structure and conventions.

Most of the sixteen tales in *Twilight Land,* originally published in *Harper's Young People* from 1889 to 1894, fall into one of three or four convenient thematic groups, with certain ones, like St. George's tale of "The Fruits of Happiness," resisting easy classification. Certain tales, including "The Stool of Fortune" and "The Salt of Life," form a group characterized by an exuberant indulgence in spells and magic, in wishes granted, in wondrous transformations. Another group, including the tales told by Cinderella and Patient Grizzle noted earlier, celebrate women and enjoin marriage. In "The Good of a Few Words," for example, a wise princess rehabilitates Beppo the Foolish, a careless spendthrift, and engineers his fortune as well as her own, in the process fomenting the overthrow of a cruel usurper to her father's throne. Again, in "Woman's Wit," a princess saves her tailor husband when, through a failure of imagination, he can no longer conjure up a task to keep a threatening demon occupied, the demon having already provided him with riches, gardens, a palace, "all that he could ask for in the world" (186). Proving the aphorism that "When man's strength fails, woman's wit prevails," the princess sends the demon, unable to straighten one of her hairs, into outer darkness, howling in frustration.

A third group of tales picks up the prevailing theme from *The Wonder Clock* of the dangers of riches, the benefits of hard work and wise moderation over luxury and reckless indulgence. In "Good Gifts and a Fool's Folly" a young spendthrift squanders his father's fortune and then hires himself out as porter to a wizard who rewards him with a cache of jewels and some good advice—"Shun thy evil companions" and "live soberly" (121). Immediately wasting this fortune and another after it with "roaring and rioting and dancing and singing" (122), the fool returns a final time to the old man who conjures for him three piles of gold from three dervishes inhabiting an iron candlestick. When the fool steals the candlestick and a magic carpet, he is given a sound drubbing by the dervishes who abandon him in a "stony desert," his obstinate profligacy suitably rewarded. "The Talisman of Solomon," another tale with the same theme, is related by Old Bidpai, who here assumes the same advisory role that he held to King Dabschelim in the *Fables,* counseling moderation and the value of honest work. The tale, a perfect diptych, concerns in its first half Aben Hassan the Wise, whose servant, the demon Zadok, shows him the fabulous treasure of the kings of Egypt, builds for him a pleasure palace, and introduces him to the beautiful but wicked Queen of the Black Isles. The talisman of Solomon, however, advises him to flee demon, treasure, palace, and sorceress, those knots in a "net of death and destruction," and to work for his living, advice he follows, leaving an enormous fortune to his son Aben Hassan the Fool. Quickly squandering this fortune and ignoring the talisman's advice to work as his father had done, Aben the Fool falls into all the traps his father had so deftly avoided, including a final catastrophe—his decapitation after opening the door promising to reveal that which would satisfy all his desires.

A final group of tales explores a related theme, offering a speculation about the nature and disposition of wealth. In "Much Shall Have More and Little Shall Have Less" a king, wishing to rule justly, sets out to discover why some folks are rich and others poor, instructing a rich man to give three hundred gold pieces to the poorest man he can find. When the money returns to the rich man three times without his striving for it, the king concludes that an incontrovertible fate determines the disposition of wealth, that the gross inequality between rich and poor is justifiable since "the way of Heaven is not to be changed" (308). This fatalistic laissez-faire attitude is reinforced in "All Things Are as Fate Wills," the story of a king who sets out to prove that "All things are as man does," only to find out that his attempts first to enrich and then to further impoverish a poor man are both frustrated by the overweening dictates of fate. A third story in this group, "Wisdom's Wages and Folly's Pay," reinforces this view of the arbitrariness of fate in bestowing riches, the wise and skillful Simon Agricola remaining poor while his foolish but lucky henchman, Babo, stumbles on great wealth. Such fatalistic, almost cynical speculations introduce a philosophical seriousness into these tales that is largely absent from those in earlier collections.

The illustrations. *Twilight Land* differs from Pyle's two preceding folktale collections in its continuous association of frame and narrative, in its exploration of subtler, often more ironic themes, and in its structural and descriptive elaborations of the usually succinct folktale form. In addition, it radically departs from its predecessors in its illustrative style. Pyle's pen-and-ink illustrations for *Twilight Land* are small, carefully focused vignettes, the depicted figures seen at greater distance than those in the earlier collections, the compositions surrounded by blank space, unbordered and unaccompanied by mottoes or captions. This absence of borders does not, however, produce the illusion that we are gazing at a snapshot of fairyland or "a sketch by our artist on the spot," effects of borderless illustrations that Tolkien condemned as "a folly and an abuse."[18] Instead, the "otherness" of

"The Pleasure Palace"
Twilight Land, 59

fairyland is suggested by Pyle's use of an evanescent, insubstantial, almost dissolving line in the illustrations, a visual equivalent of the thin, tenuous voices the narrator describes as characterizing those who speak in Twilight Land (336). These airy illustrations in what Henry Pitz calls Pyle's "impressionist" style are used to greatest effect in those tales with Oriental settings. In "The Talisman of Solomon," for example, the illustrations, suggestive and evocative rather than directly declarative, are nevertheless highly articulated, coalescing style and subject in a perfect harmony. The depiction of the jewel room presided over by the golden statues (55) is a shimmery, light-filled dream-vision, the translucence emanating from the jewels dissolving the solid arches and stone walls of the underground vault and casting wispy shadows behind Aben the Fool and the demon Zadok. The same insubstantiality characterizes the pleasure palace (59), its radiant domes and minarets hovering in the thin air of fairyland and glittering like a fata morgana. Like the illustrations for "The Talisman of Solomon," those for "Woman's Wit" shimmer with glowing gems, diaphanous gowns, gleaming metals, and light-pierced shadows. In one of the most stunning illustrations in this tale (189) Pyle economically portrays the malevolent power of the demon with a dense thicket of curvilinear lines from which extrudes the suggestion of a face and limbs. Slashed sketchily onto the page, the demon overwhelms the clearly representational figure of the tailor kneeling before him. The concluding illustration (193) features a replication of crescents—leg, arms, wing, moon—issuing from a series of pen-scratches representing the conquered demon dissolving into darkness.

Thus Pyle discontinues the completely outlined contour drawings placed within fully defined settings so characteristic of the illustrations for *Pepper & Salt* and *The Wonder Clock*. Indeed, the pictures for *Twilight Land* are synecdochic notations or shorthand depictions meant to suggest a larger scene without delineating it fully, the most obvious examples being crowd scenes (179, 245, 269) consisting simply of a focal point surrounded by a jumble of nearly disembodied heads arranged along a slant-axis spatial perspective. Other excellent examples of this synecdochic style may be found in "Not a Pin to Choose" where the cave Abdallah enters is represented by little more than a large, irregular black smudge on an otherwise blank page (271), and in "Ill-Luck and the Fiddler" where the fiddler falls into an apple tree, represented with the greatest economy by a cluster of scribbled leaves and globes and by several wavy lines suggesting a tree bole (91). This last illustration, and others like it (10, 51, 183, 315, for example) are placed on the page coadjacent to the running text so as to be visible peripherally as one reads.

Pyle's rich illustrative inventiveness in the book also manifests itself in his intricate play with perspective in "Ill-Luck and the Fiddler," especially in the illustration depicting the three great marble basins containing gold, silver, and jewels, the shimmering surfaces of which spread diagonally across the page, ending with a glimpse of the old man and the amazed fiddler crouching in the background (85). In a preceding illustration (81) Ill-Luck flies with the fiddler into the inner depths of the page to a house just barely perceptible in the distance. Set on an otherwise blank white sheet, this "flying picture," along with a similar one in "A Piece of Good Luck" (231), captures perfectly the giddy pendulousness of the hanging figures. Such illustrations help to make *Twilight Land* one of the most visually sophisticated of all of Pyle's works for juveniles.

Twilight Land evidences the strain Pyle apparently began to feel at the restrictions imposed on him by the succinct folktale formulas learned from his earlier use of the source narratives in Grimm and Jacobs and by the artistic conventions for depicting fairyland that he himself had codified in his illustrations for the two preceding collections. *Twilight Land* thus reflects Pyle's transition to the writing of longer literary romances, often for adults, and the adaptation of his illustrative style to the requirements of this genre as well as to the growing contemporary demand for halftone and color reproductions then being made available by rapid advances in photographic printing techniques. For these reasons, the transitional *Twilight Land* received lukewarm appraisals from Henry Pitz and Charles Abbott, Pyle's most prominent critics, who found it lacking in "the intimacy and enfolding quality" as well as in "the inspiration" and "fairy-tale zest" of the two preceding collections.[19] Judged on its own narrative and pictorial merits, however, and not in comparison to works from which it pointedly deviates, *Twilight Land* should assume a greater distinction in Pyle's canon than it has previously been accorded.

A Modern Aladdin (1892)

Originally serialized in *Harper's Bazaar* from May to July 1891 and written at the same time as certain of the *Twilight Land* folktales, *A Modern Aladdin* is what Northrup Frye would call a "sentimental romance," a work characterized by an extended literary development of the formulas and conventions of the folktale, or "naive romance." According to Frye, the energy of sentimental romance is generated by a constant gravitational pull between two worlds, one above and the other below the realm of ordinary experience. The first, an "idyllic world," is associated with "happiness, security, and peace," its images being "spring and summer, flowers and sunshine." The other, a "demonic or night world," is a locus of trials and adventures involving "separation, loneliness, humiliation, pain, and the threat of more pain."[20] *A Modern Aladdin* involves a series of dizzying ascents and descents between these two worlds, its plot an ebb and flow of mystery and resolution, a rhythm of tension and release, darkness and vision, a wavering between dream and nightmare.

The work's prologue introduces the mysterious Comte de St.-Germaine, reputed to be the richest man in the world and to have lived for five hundred years, his sudden and unexplained disappearance from the Parisian scene occasioning even more speculation than had his meteoric arrival. During the course of the narrative the comte's identity, history, and eventual fate gradually become clear as he interacts with Oliver Munier, at the beginning of the story a "poor, ignorant, dull" lad of eighteen, "a witless, idle sot, satisfied to sit the day through on the bench in front of the inn."[21] A typical unregenerated folktale hero, malleable and in the process of becoming, Oliver receives his call to adventure from the comte, who, as in the original Aladdin tale, claims to be Oliver's long-lost uncle, in Pyle's version lately returned from the Americas ostensibly to share his fabulous diamonds with Oliver. Mysteries soon amass like moths after sunset. A moonlit woman, her keening compared to the wailing of cats, appears below Oliver's window as if in warning. The victim of an elaborate ruse, Oliver is fetched away to Paris simply to secure for the comte and his odd, wizened servant Gaspard two mysterious phials from an underground apartment, a mission which for some enigmatic reason they themselves cannot perform. Once in Paris, Oliver enters the cellar-apartment where, lost in a cloud of unknowing, he stumbles about among moldering luxuries and comes upon the desiccated corpse of a young woman before finding the elixirs he is sent to retrieve. Act 1, then, involves a gradual engendering of suspense, an increasing distillation of tension as Oliver, a naive victim crouching before his captors "like a rabbit before the face of a serpent" (25), descends to the "demonic world," a macabre landscape of thrilling horrors, the often-repeated image for which is nightmare, a struggling in the black waters of sleep.

Oliver's growing sense of self precipitates his ascent from the demonic world. Refusing to hand over the elixirs until his safety is assured, he is locked in the underground rooms from which he is saved by following a cat—another embodiment of the moonlit woman?—through an air shaft to the surface. Intercepted by Gaspard, he is conducted to the comte's gold-and-white apartments into which he enters as if stepping "from the threshold of one world into another" (56). Oliver's loss of innocence through his confrontation with horror and his growth through trial give him the right to demand an understanding of the demonic world into which he has been plunged. Having gained "wisdom, shrewdness, cunning," and "power" (59) as a result of his trial, Oliver now refuses to play victim, threatening to dash the bottles out of a window unless all mysteries are resolved. The comte's long inset alchemical tale of the corruption, sin, and ultimate sorrow attendant upon those mortals who aspire to immortality and unlimited wealth works as a hinge to the plot diptych, resolving the tensions engendered by the romance's initial knot of mysteries. But this resolution only serves to introduce a new set of tensions upon which Pyle structures the second half of his plot. For instance, the comte reveals in his long monologue that he sought to immure Oliver in order to save himself from an astrologically predicted downfall at Oliver's hands. Accordingly, he gives Oliver a cache of diamonds on condition that he never return to Paris.

Enriched, newly instructed in drawing-room etiquette, now actor rather than victim, "Oliver de Monnière" returns to his village to woo Celeste, the Marquis de Flourens's daughter, his opulent diamonds granting him access to an "idyllic world" of gilded summer houses, flowery gardens, and Celeste's pure heart. In spite of these dramatic surface transformations, however, Oliver has not yet become like those self-controlled and self-determining heroes everywhere met in fairy-tale conclusions who wield the power of their full majority. His second descent into the demonic world is occasioned by his again becoming a pawn, this time resigning his will and fortunes to the marquis, who insists that Oliver accompany the family to Paris. There the couple is celebrated at Madame de Pompadour's salon as a new Corydon and Phyllis, harbingers of a returned Arcadia.

The comte saves his revenge for the broken vow until Oliver's wedding night, plunging him from the heights of the idyllic world to the darkest depths of the demonic when he abducts Celeste, dissolves Oliver's diamonds, ruins his reputation, and orders him to drown himself in the Seine. His will mastered by the comte, Oliver is saved from a parapet by the mysterious moonlit woman and, in a grotesque denouement, reduces the comte, that demonic infiltrator into the idyllic world of the eighteenth-century drawing room, to an ancient mass of dried skin and bones when he crushes his vial of immortality in a struggle, the comte's borrowed body being stripped from him by the ghoulish Gaspard. Free at last, Oliver returns to the marquis's country estates, his ventures into the idyllic world concluded by the loss of his fabulous wealth and his plunges into the demonic world ended with the comte's death. Like a fairy-tale hero, Oliver returns after his tutelary trials to the ordinary world newly equipped for happiness and success there. With the release of the tensions aroused in the romance's second half comes the resolution of the central mystery of the comte's necromantic identity and sudden disappearance introduced in the prologue. The conclusion rings the curtain down with a tidy dismissal of actors and audience to the real world that Oliver himself has entered.

The reader, then, dances through *A Modern Aladdin* to two discordant but counterpointing tunes—flight and dalliance, nightmare and reverie. These divergent effects—the orderly civility of drawing room and garden and the melodramatic emotional chaos of the cavern and the comte's apartments—are counterpoised, brought into balance and meaningful relation in Pyle's carefully crafted plot. To complement these alternating rhythms and to enflesh the bare bones of the romance's folktale original, Pyle infuses aristocratic, "idyllic" elements from the ultra-refined eighteenth-century France of Louis XV as well as "demonic" conventions from nineteenth-century bourgeois melodrama, aptly calling the eclectic mix an "extravaganza."

Pyle employs dreamy Watteau-esque settings, pictorial references to the commedia dell'arte, and luxurious Louis Quinze trappings for the love idyll. Set during "the gay butterfly days of La Pompadour," the romance is narrated in a style suiting the "polished surface" of the age it portrays (3), the dialogue capturing the elegantly modulated conversation and heightened sensibilities of its aristocratic characters. Opulently described settings include the mirror-paneled drawing rooms and glimmering nymph-statued gardens depicted by Watteau, an artist specifically invoked in the second half of the narrative, during much of which Oliver-in-love drifts about "in the bewildering glamour of a golden dream" (139) like the lovers in Watteau's *A Pilgrimage to Cythera*. Pyle pays homage to Watteau in certain of his illustrations as well as in his verbal depictions. The illustration showing the marquis in bed (114), for example, captures all the effervescent play of light and shadow on silk brocade, lace, and damasked arras that so delighted that painter; and in the several illustrations (130, 140) depicting Oliver and Celeste strolling in a garden "such as Watteau loved to paint" (129), Celeste wears a "Watteau-gown" and Oliver the garb of one of the gentleman lovers in the eighteenth-century artist's *fêtes galantes*. Oliver, however, dons this gentlemanly garb only after he has saved himself from the horrors of the underground chamber and wrested from the comte a share of his great diamond fortune. In earlier illustrations the dreamy, gullible Oliver is always portrayed as a Pierrot or Gilles, the figure Watteau painted obsessively toward the end of his short life.

In an adroit reference to Watteau and a graceful acknowledgment of the vogue enjoyed by the commedia dell'arte in eighteenth-century France, Pyle divides *A Modern Aladdin* into acts and scenes just as if it were to be performed at the *Comédie Italienne* by those stock commedia figures—Pierrot, Il Dottore, Pantalone, the lovers—used here in his illustrations to depict his major characters. An early illustration (12), for example, shows Oliver, outfitted in Pierrot's baggy white blouse and pants, conversing with the comte, clothed entirely in black and thus resembling, at least physically, the foolish and pedantic Dottore. Listening to their conversation is Gaspard, described as having "a long, sharp chin that stuck out like that of a punchinello" (15), the clever and often nasty servant in the commedia. During the course of the narrative, Oliver transforms himself from a Pierrot to an Orazio or a Leandro, becoming a witty and capable lover worthy of his Isabella or Flaminia, in this case Celeste, daughter of that Pantalone figure, the marquis. Most of these characters, however, bear only physical resemblances to their commedia counterparts, their personalities, with a few exceptions, not directly corresponding.

Offsetting the "golden ether" (140) and all the rococo Louis Quinze embellishments of the love idyll are the nineteenth-century melodramatics of the dark adventures in the demonic realm, including charged settings and atmospherics, violent stimuli, and vehement emotional reactions. Again, certain illustrations in the work provide an index to these nightmarish effects. The macabre atmosphere of the moldy underground rooms, for example, is perfectly captured in the illustration at page 36: the lantern Oliver holds discloses the skeletonized corpse before him, while the shadow looming behind him duplicates and intensifies his carefully delineated terror. One of the most successful illustrations in this series depicts Oliver cowering just inside the

underground doorway as the comte and Gaspard caper in their impo-
tent fury to reach him on the other side of the red line, a boundary
they cannot cross, "tossing their hooked, claw-like hands in the air,
foaming with rage, snarling and gnashing like wolves" (42). These
depictions capture the distortions of human faces upon which strong
light has suddenly flared (30, 84), the fearful shadows cast in an ill-lit
landscape of terror (22, 42), and the dissolution of solid objects by
which one usually orients oneself in the world (94, 198). Reminiscent
of the "impressionistic" illustrations in *Twilight Land,* these depictions
are always expressive, always economical, Oliver's sense of entrapment
in the cavern (46), for example, powerfully suggested by a minimal,
smudgelike shape of enclosing darkness on the blank page, only Oliver's head and upturned face emerging from the devouring shadows.
These illustrations, pregnant with emotional chaos, balance the sunlit
gardens and candle-lit drawing rooms of the idyllic illustrations, the
whole a fitting complement to the rhythms of darkness and light,
dream and nightmare governing the plot.

Just as Pyle evicts his readers from fairyland at some point in each
of his three folktale collections, so in *A Modern Aladdin* he ushers them
out of the realm of the mysterious and fantastic, escorting them back-
stage in "After the Play" to show the extravaganza's pasteboard scenery
folded up and the actors washing the paint off their faces. Back in the
real world, he speculates about the identity of the mysterious moonlit
woman, concluding that she must have been the better life of the
comte materialized unavoidably along with his evil life. Thus Pyle
concludes this long tale as he had many shorter ones—with a moral
tag. It is difficult to disagree with Robert Louis Stevenson, author of
similar, though shorter romances in the *New Arabian Nights,* who
thought *A Modern Aladdin* "capital fun," but who concluded that Pyle
should have omitted the terminal moral speculation, leaving "his bogey tale a bogey tale, and a good one at that."[22]

The Price of Blood (1899)

A *jeu,* a bagatelle, *The Price of Blood* (first published in *Collier's Weekly,* 17 December 1898), ironically called by Pyle a "serious story," is
freighted with a moral ponderous for its slender frame. In his preface
Pyle offers this slight but absorbing thriller as a stimulus to lead "the
thoughtful mind to consider how easy it is for the innocent to become
entangled in a fate which in no wise concerns him, and for the discreet

to become enveloped in a network of circumstances which he himself has had no part in framing."[23] *The Price of Blood* tells the story of Nathaniel Griscombe's nightmare involvement with the Desmond brothers, fomenters of a bloody revolution in "Industan," who are hounded to horrible retribution by the potentate they have overthrown.

Unlike *A Modern Aladdin,* a fantasy evaporated with the ringing down of a curtain, *The Price of Blood* is presented as "true," the introduction establishing New York in 1807 as cosmopolitan enough to harbor a deposed East Indian rajah who, from his court on Broadway, pursues a terrible vengeance. Like *A Modern Aladdin,* however, *The Price of Blood* is an "extravaganza," a "sentimental romance," an elaboration of fairy-tale formulas and conventions, presenting as its protagonist an untried, indolent young attorney with inner resources who traverses a demonic landscape scattered with caskets of jewels, harrowing adventures, and characters in outlandish costumes, all set in a carefully structured plot concluding with the protagonist's idyllic marriage and undreamt-of success.

In chapter 1 Nathaniel Griscombe receives an abrupt call to adventure during a riotous meeting of the "Bluebird Club" attended by an assemblage of rakes attired in wild costumes. Dressed in a cocked hat and "in the loose cotton blouse and drawers of a clown" (20), he is called from the midst of mayhem to accompany a man cloaked and masked in black, who identifies himself as a Mr. Desmond, announces that he is under a death warrant, and commissions Griscombe to warn his brother in Bordentown, N.J., and to carry there a casket of jewels stolen during the revolution. In this chapter Pyle thus blends two heightened and extravagant orders of reality, confronting a clown with the ominous and grotesque, the first of the startling conjoinings composing the tale. *The Price of Blood,* a tapestry of macabre coincidents and juxtapositions, strives throughout for strong effects, for startling estrangements from the ordinary and familiar.

Chapter 2 opens with Griscombe's return to his rooms from breakfast after a night "disturbed by vivid and diabolical visions of terror" (39). Awaiting him is a second client, an exotic, yellow-faced, hooknosed foreigner incongruously dressed as a dandy in "the latest cut of fashion" (41). In grotesquely formal speech this apparition offers him a hundred twenty-dollar gold pieces—exactly the retainer received from Desmond—to play him a game of jackstraws. A bit of comic deflation, a discordant absurdity, the game also serves as an apt image for the entanglement in which Griscombe finds himself. After dallying with Griscombe "as a cat dallies with a mouse" (46), the jackstraw player abruptly departs, leaving the attorney relieved to discover that the casket of jewels remains hidden beneath his bed. In the next chapter Griscombe descends the nightmare spiral a full rotation when, arriving in Bordentown at the house of Desmond's brother and partner in the murder of a prince and a queen during the revolution they direct, the two open the casket to find Desmond's face reposing amidst the jewels, a diamond, "like a tear," resting on a cheek and a priceless ruby clinging to "the pallid and sphinx-like lips," the forehead banded with the warning "YOU NEXT" (58). Enmeshed in this macabre violence and intrigue is Arabella Desmond, "one of the most perfect beauties in the United States" (53), a young woman of "hermit-like seclusion from the world" (54), "innocent, beautiful, radiantly unconscious" of the terrors surrounding her (60). Wishing to protect her, Griscombe cannot disentangle himself from the affair and is thus drawn deeper into the spiral of horrors at the same time that his growing love for Arabella initiates a countering gyre toward nuptial joy, she being "a bright and radiant vision" shining in the gloom (67). Thus he agrees to convey Arabella and her father's jewel casket to safety in New York, retaining the exact same fee from his third client as he had obtained from the previous two.

A fourth client awaits him at an inn in Newark, an ancient man with a long white beard and serpent eyes who offers him the now-familiar fee to play tit-tat-toe, a game again emblematic of the web through which Griscombe must make his way. The tale culminates when, arriving in New York late on Christmas Eve in an impenetrable snowstorm, Griscombe and Arabella are fetched to confront at last the dethroned rajah, that "spider who had woven all this web of mystery" (87). After Arabella opportunely faints away, the rajah opens the jewel casket to reveal the two faces of the Desmonds, "so exactly alike that they might have been cast in the same mould" (91). Over each is scattered in mockery a shower of jewels, the price of the blood they have shed during the revolution. Though intending a "different fate" for Arabella, the avenged potentate agrees to hand her over to Griscombe as a reward for his unwitting services. Sprung from the demonic spiral, Griscombe circles upward in the idyllic gyre, becoming Arabella's protector, then her husband, and in 1850 head of the New York Bar. Like the protagonists of Pyle's pirate tales, most notably those in *Within the*

Capes and *The Ruby of Kishmoor,* Griscombe returns from his youthful descent into the demonic to lead a long, prosperous, and uneventful life.

In *The Price of Blood,* a parody of the sentimental romance, Pyle pushes romantic conventions to their limits and beyond, amusing himself with characters exotic and grotesque, dialogue stilted in its incongruous formality, situations dependent upon excessive coincidence and the intrusion of the wondrous into the ordinary, a plot as honed and spare as a geometrical design, conjoinings and juxtapositions startling in their unexpectedness, a palette of jeweled colors gleaming fitfully from a dark canvas, and a hero and heroine who have traveled express from fairyland via nineteenth-century melodrama. The introduction and conclusion set the ironic tone with an understated admission that this perfectly outlandish story "may at times appear a little strange and out of the ordinary course of events" (13) and with a commendation of the "serious" reader who "will not be inclined to disbelieve that which has been so soberly narrated, even though it cause him some surprise that such things should have occurred in the midst of sedate American towns" (97). The six halftone illustrations, exercises in racial stereotyping, depict sinister but whimsical Asians in earrings and turbans peeking around corners and from behind curtains or sitting cross-legged and inscrutable on cushions. As Henry Pitz put it, *The Price of Blood* is "Pyle letting go with a will"; [24] it is an extravagant indulgence in the conventions governing the fairy tale and the sentimental romance.

The Garden Behind the Moon (1895)

Like *A Modern Aladdin* and *The Price of Blood, The Garden Behind the Moon* takes its form and central motifs from the fairy tale, opening, for example, with the formulaic "Once upon a time," featuring an immature hero in the process of becoming, and chronicling the trials he must undergo with the aid of semimagical helpers in order to win his princess and to enter into his full estate at work's end. Unlike *A Modern Aladdin* and *The Price of Blood,* however, *The Garden Behind the Moon* does not parlay these fairy tale conventions into the sentimental romance. Instead, the work is an allegorical myth, a "true fairy story,"[25] the kind that "wise people and little children would rather read . . . than anything else" (192). In *The Garden* Pyle attempts to resolve into a coherent whole the metaphysical speculations occasioned by the death of his young son Sellers in 1889, his continued reading of the mystic Swedenborg, and his correspondence during the early 1890s with W. D. Howells, then also grieving over the loss of a child. Borrowing, among other elements, the pre-Freudian box and key imagery from George MacDonald's *The Golden Key* (1864), Nanny's moon-dream and Diamond's journey through death from MacDonald's *At the Back of the North Wind* (1871), and the colloquial tone and evolutionary vision from Charles Kingsley's *The Water Babies* (1863), Pyle strives in *The Garden Behind the Moon* to pierce the deceptiveness of the mundane, to delve beneath appearances in order to understand not only the post-mortem spirit world and its hierarchies but also the purpose and meaning of life itself.

Such an understanding demands a perspective other than the one afforded by the physical senses, a wisdom beyond worldly knowledge, an imaginative penetration through ordinary common sense, a faith transcending earthly rationality. To gain this perspective on earth one must "get behind the Moon-Angel," there to see things "turned top-syturvy" (103), to see "men walk on their heads instead of their heels," "trees grow upside down," and "wise men talk nonsense" until, after cracking "through the crust of things" at death, one is able to get back "into the Land of Right-side-up again" (105). Such persistent estrangements from accustomed ways of seeing, such radical reversals of vision penetrate Pyle's tale. Its hero, "Silly" David, is seen by everyone, including his parents, as a simpleton, a mooncalf; yet it is David who "can see more through the square hole of a millstone than t'other side of it" (34), who perceives the Moon-Angel making "old things over into new things" (71), not as a figure of terror, but "in his true shape, with his face shining brightly, and his hair flowing" (35). Hans Krout is also a figure of derision in worldly eyes; yet it is Hans who knows more about moon-lore than anyone else and who, after the disappointment of his worldly hopes, aspires to less transient goals, becoming "the only wise man" among those who think him crazy (181). Compared to David and Hans, those whom the world holds wise show themselves fools when seen from this reversed perspective, especially the "scientist with two-pair of short-sighted spectacles on his nose" writing the "great book upon the differentiation of Human Reason" and his fellow "with far-sighted glasses" counting microbes in a cubic inch of buttermilk (9). In perhaps the most telling inversion of all,

Pyle assures such "wise folks" intent on dismissing his tale as nonsense that "sometimes there is more solid truth in a little nonsense than in a whole peck of potatoes" (59).

Correct vision allows one to see the inside rather than simply the illusory outside of things, a redeeming perception alleviating fear and despair through the discernment of a kindly providence sustaining all existence. Thus, according to the narrator, most people are dreadfully afraid of the moon-house, associated as it is with death, because "they only see the outside of it, and do not know what is within" (44). Granted a clearer vision, the narrator himself now recognizes the moon-house as "a calm, beautiful, lovely place" rather than the "great white emptiness" of his earlier nightmares (45). Through the second-story windows of the moon-house, David, too, is granted a clear insight into a universal benevolence penetrating and dissolving earthly cruelty. Consequently, his horrifying glimpse of the African trader throwing a dead slave and her living baby overboard from a slave ship is immediately dispelled by a vision of these martyrs ushered by the Moon-Angel into a region of dazzling light where they are welcomed extravagantly by "thousands and thousands of voices, singing in a multitudinous cadence" (54). Though David learns that grotesque human cruelty is no more to the inside of an event "than the shell of the egg is to the meat" (55), he still asks the Man-in-the-moon why there must be such a cruel outside, the old man replying that "the more sad the outside, the more beautiful almost always is the inside" (56). David's "inside" vision grows so keen that his glimpse of a rich tropical rain forest through the moon-window reveals the benign evolutionary processes of the forest working "with all its might and main to get things in such order that man might live there some day" (63). The transforming power of this inside view emancipates from anxiety and dread all those who share it, revealing to them the true nature of death as well as the rectifying force of divine justice ever operative beneath the often harsh surface of events.

In addition to presenting this renewed spiritual vision, this redeeming double perspective, *The Garden Behind the Moon* explores the afterlife bestowed on those who die in innocence as well as the tasks confronting those who experience the world full term. In a letter to an acquaintance Pyle notes that his story, being a serious attempt to penetrate the dark glass through which mortals see, is necessarily tinged with a "certain indefinable mystery,"[26] an elusiveness inescapably contingent upon mystical speculation. Thus, the work is replete with references to intuitional perception rather than rational certainty, its arresting images suffused with multiple and indefinite significances. A central emblem for the elusive quality in the work is the star the Moon-Angel gazes at so steadfastly, clearly visible in peripheral vision, but dimming when stared at directly. When we try to think about why the Moon-Angel gazes at this star, says the narrator, "then we cannot tell; when we do not try to think about it, then we know all about it" (87). Thus *The Garden Behind the Moon* cannot be reduced to simple allegory. Myth and symbol its métier, the work's meaning is conveyed through suggestion and intuition. To enter Pyle's *Garden,* a reader must follow the advice given Tangle in MacDonald's *Golden Key* when she contemplates the dark hole she must enter to find the Old Man of the Fire: "You must throw yourself in. There is no other way."[27]

This is not to suggest, however, that the work is vague or indecipherable. Endowed with a clear diptych structure like many of the extended fairy tales of *Twilight Land* and the subsequent romances, *The Garden Behind the Moon* opens with David's journey to the moon-house, his work there in polishing the stars, and his subsequent holidays in the moon-garden, "the best place out of the world in which to play" (71), an Edenic garden of innocent delights reserved for those from three to twelve years old who depart from this life before their minds and faculties are yet developed. According to Pyle, this garden shelters his dead son, referred to in the book's introduction as "the little boy whom I loved the best of all" (3). There, David, no longer derided as a mooncalf, is made king by the children and romps with them, his innocent heart swelling "so full of happiness that it almost ached" (81). David, however, has left his clothes on earth so that "nobody down there knows otherwise than that [he is] in them" (47). Thus, not yet dead, he cannot remain in the moon-garden for long. Before his ascent to the moon-house after his first visit to the garden, he meets a little princess, Phyllis, and vows to marry her someday, rejoining her and his other friends in this idyllic garden for three days each month until his twelfth birthday.

The second half of the book details David's life-quest, beginning with his unhappy expulsion from the garden with the explanation that "innocent little children must grow into men and women who are not innocent" (97). To initiate his redeeming quest for the Wonder-Box and the Know-All Book, which lie in the Iron Castle of the Iron Man, David must get behind the Moon-Angel, whose now-terrifying visage precipitates in him a startling change of perspective: the golden dream of the idyllic garden dims to nightmare "in which there was something of terror and darkness" (107), a frustrating stasis, a captivity, and a bondage. His death to childhood innocence occurs during his passage through the frost and fire of the Moon-Angel, on the other side of whom he finds, "with a sudden shock of wonder," that he has grown into a man. The mysterious old woman with a red petticoat whom he meets hanging out clothes to dry, the "snowy white and fluttering" souls of men grown soiled by use in the world, spins for him a revisionist myth of the primal garden where Eve and Adam, "the innocent woman and innocent man," lived without sorrow, but without joy or delight, until the Moon-Angel bestows on them the gift of an iron box in which is locked "the greatest joy and the greatest sorrow in the world" (119). Forsaking their childish innocence and deciding that "surely it is worth suffering the greatest sorrow for the sake of the greatest joy" (120)—a decision the adult David applauds—Eve and Adam open the box but are so frightened by the great cloud of terror billowing forth that they flee in panic, forsaking the attendant joy. When David arrives at the Iron Castle, "a great dark, grim place," he sees the Iron Man holding the Know-All Book upside down, attempting but forever unable to read it. Trying to escape from the giant after stealing the book, box, and golden key, David hears Phyllis, captive in the Iron Castle, calling to be freed from the moon-garden. Startled into a sudden recognition that what was garden to innocent eyes is now prison to the mature eyes of experience, David rescues Phyllis from her entrapment, slays the Iron Man, and escapes to the moon-house with the treasure. Back on earth, they find in the Know-All Book countless permutations of the same message: that in their marriage they will find the greatest joy possible to them, the joy with which all true fairy tales end, that "true marriage joy" at the heart of the Swedenborgian cosmology imaged for Pyle in the mystical marriage of the "yellow heaven" and the "brown earth" (191) from which all creation springs.

Thus the saving double perspective granted throughout the book— "inside" versus "outside" vision, imagination versus fact, faith versus reason—undergirds the plot structure of the whole. What is complete fulfillment for those who die to the world while still in their original innocence is bondage for those matured through their experience of it. The garden of the first half of the book and the Iron Castle of the second are thus the same place, seen respectively through the Blakean perspectives of innocence and experience. *The Garden Behind the Moon* radiates with Pyle's benign, hopeful vision of an encompassing joy hedging the universe round, a joy freely bestowed on those who die young and generously made available to those in the world who seek it.

The line drawings and halftone illustrations perfectly complement the initial dreamy innocence and later heroic action of the tale's two parts. The foreward headpiece, for example, depicts the Moon-Angel in the garden sheltering a little boy between his outstretched arms and under his bright wings (1). Rose-garlanded, his face shadowed but mysteriously underlit, the Moon-Angel resembles the angel-jester in the frontispiece to *Twilight Land* in all but that angel's belled cap, a detail inappropriate for the more serious presiding spirit of this "true fairy tale." *Twilight Land*'s introduction headpiece is also echoed in *The Garden*'s decorative band for chapter 2 (9), both depicting a pipe-playing angel leading a group of merry children in the moonlight. The full-page halftones, however, signal a departure from the Land of Fancy, locus for *Pepper & Salt* and *The Wonder Clock*. In *The Garden*'s frontispiece, for example, David and Phyllis, rendered in oil in a more rounded, three-dimensional form than is ever achieved in the flat pen drawings of the earlier fairy-tale collections, stand on a graveled garden path among roses pendulous with dew, their eyes deep and dilated with the "inside" vision that sets them apart from the world. Again, the illustration of David walking with Hans through knots of derisive townsfolk (25) captures the moon-gaze, startling and otherworldly, of those able to see through the outside of things. The dreamy, static quality of innocence captured in these initial illustrations gives way to the heroic vigor and activity of the illustrations in the book's second half, including the depiction of David wrestling with the winged horse (133) and his triumphant slaying of the Iron Man (163). The concluding illustration is an epithalamion, depicting David and the princess at front center, looming heroically large over the backgrounded nobles of the court (189).

Of equal importance in Pyle's careful visual expression of the work's central themes are the decorative pen-and-ink chapter headpieces that depict the often paradoxical workings of the Moon-Angel. The illustration at the head of chapter 3, for example, picturing the Angel directing a heavily laden pilgrim out of his dark way into a sunlit land, is countered by the illustration at the head of chapter 5, depicting a woman, her children, and a companion starting in terror at the Angel's sudden apparition. Subsequent illustrations show the Angel leading David to the moon-window (44) or David and Phyllis to the moon-

"In the Garden Behind the Moon"
The Garden Behind the Moon, frontispiece

garden (84), and, after their loss of innocence, away from those places (91, 159). Finally, at the head of chapter 10, the Moon-Angel, a fiery specter, holds a scythe and an hourglass in his outstretched arms, emblems of the blighting awareness of death and time that accompanies David's loss of innocence; and at the head of the concluding chapter, the Angel, now transfigured in radiant light, holds out two laurel wreaths, emblems of David's heroic victory over those twin terrors. These illustrations combine with the text to make Pyle's effulgent *Garden* a serious and engaging work worthy of better than the all-but-complete obscurity into which it has fallen. Unlike the similar fantasies of MacDonald and Kingsley on which *The Garden* is modeled, Pyle's work has long been out of print, perhaps because of a continuing bias toward British over American writers for children. As Perry Nodelman suggests in a recent article, Pyle's *Garden*, "a fascinating and too much neglected novel," deserves careful critical reconsideration.[28]

Chapter Four

Heroes and Adventurers:
Popular Historical Fiction

The 1880s and 1890s saw a renewed interest in the historical romance rivaling the great popular enthusiasm for the works of Sir Walter Scott and James Fenimore Cooper in the first half of the century. H. S. Canby, an astute observer of turn-of-the-century America, notes that this "new American school of the historical romance rose over night, blossomed like the desert in April, and withered at the first touch of twentieth-century realism," but not before these romances became such significant "determinants of inner life" for contemporary readers that no one unfamiliar with them "will ever understand the America of that day."[1] So avid were readers for these romances that by 1900, according to F. L. Mott, five of the ten best-sellers on the *Bookman's* list were historical novels. "History," he notes, "was coming alive—the history of Rome and knighthood and the French Revolution and (best of all) the history of the American Revolution and the American pioneers— and how the American reading public loved it all!"[2] According to Canby, a rediscovery of American history did much to precipitate this fad, for as soon as the popular novelists began "to create a romantic Colonial America the intoxication began. . . . Suddenly we became aware of a past—our own—that seemed as good as Scott's, and much like it."[3]

Into this floodtide of historical romance flowed a tributary stream of nineteenth-century "boy literature," the product of what Gillian Avery calls "the late Victorian vogue for manly boys," a literature of historical adventure dedicated to the formation of the *mens sana in corpore sano*, the boy with "pluck." As Avery notes, "long before girls were allowed amusing books, boys had their Marryat and Ballantyne," Mayne Reid, Henty, Manville Fenn, and Westerman, as well as *The Boy's Own Paper* (1879–1963) with its adventure serials and cliff-hangers about warriors, pirates, heroes, and explorers.[4]

Ever a man of his time, Pyle launched a literary barque on the confluence of these two streams, producing historical adventure romances for adolescents, several involving knights and robber barons in medieval Europe and others involving pirates, planters, and merchants in colonial and early nineteenth-century America. Pyle's attitude toward adventure in these romances was essentially ambiguous: while he relished it as a vivifying intermission in the quotidian, he nevertheless saw it as undermining the steady regimen of work and duty he persistently championed in his fiction and in his personal life. In his adventure romances, however, he could unite the hegira with the antithetical hearth, the Odyssean with the Telemachean impulses, by allowing his heroes to follow for a brief time the dangerous and irresponsible siren call to adventure before returning to the cozy domestic world of obligation and accountability. Undoubtedly he thus recognized the essential function of the historical adventure novel as a safe way for the homebound into perilous and fascinating realms, a vicarious plunge into terror, risk, tension, and uncertainty without the loss of order, security, the familiar and predictable. As John G. Cawelti says of popular formula fiction in general, Pyle's adventure romances, especially his pirate tales, enable his audience "to explore in fantasy the boundary between the permitted and the forbidden and to experience in a carefully controlled way the possibility of stepping across this boundary," of indulging curiosity about actions feckless, unruly, or subversive "without endangering the cultural patterns that reject them."[5] Though Pyle, aware of the rising tide of realism, attempted one novel in that vein, *Rejected of Men,* his heart and talents were clearly allied with Robert Louis Stevenson and the historical adventure romance.

In this chapter *Otto of the Silver Hand* and *Men of Iron,* both set in medieval Europe, receive primary consideration as the best of Pyle's historical adventures and the only ones that can claim a wide readership. They are both still in print, unlike the pirate romances discussed after them. The chapter concludes with a consideration of Pyle's only realist novel.

Otto of the Silver Hand (1888)

One of the first historical novels written for children by an American, *Otto of the Silver Hand* is set in the Middle Ages at the pivotal point when Rudolph of Hapsburg forges a federation of lawless German barons into a viable empire, thus transforming chaos into order, barbarism into civil accord. Eschewing the highly romanticized view of the Middle Ages then in vogue for a depiction closer to Twain's bleak but more precise vision in *A Connecticut Yankee in King Arthur's Court* (1889), Pyle attempts in *Otto* a realistic portrayal of the medieval period as "a great black gulf in human history, a gulf of ignorance, of superstition, of cruelty, and of wickedness."[6] Accordingly, he sets his story in an atmosphere of grim castles, ruthless baronial robbers, brutalized peasants, mutilation and sudden death, and intersecting cycles of revenge, but illuminates this "dreadful period in our world's history" with the sweet and ultimately triumphant presences of those "few good men and women here and there . . . who preserved and tenderly cared for the truths that the dear Christ taught, and lived and died for in Palestine so long ago" (2). In the best tradition of the historical novel Pyle allows his readers to penetrate the intimate life of the thirteenth century, to "in-dwell" there through an unsparing presentation of the historical data— human actions, manners, customs, details of daily living, habits of thought and language—that enflesh that world, rendering it paradoxically both alien and familiar to readers fixed in the present. In *Otto of the Silver Hand,* then, Pyle populates an accurately portrayed historical period with fictional characters and events to reflect the timeless opposition between good and evil, forgiveness and revenge, charitable reason and brutal coercion. The book is an influential one in the history of children's literature because, as Henry C. Pitz notes, it makes a "clean break" with the then "prevailing reluctance of writers to deal with brutality and evil in books for children," being published "at a time when, with only the fewest exceptions, children's authors timidly circled away from the bitterness of life or threw a veil over it."[7]

Otto of the Silver Hand is a thematic tension of opposites, a dialectic between light and darkness, order and anarchy. Its plot is filled with rapid, often violent action, packed with the "brute incident" Robert Louis Stevenson saw as a crucial element in all successful adventure romance. Raised by the gentle monks of St. Michaelsburg, twelve-year-old Otto is fetched home to the grim Castle Drachenhausen by his robber baron father, Conrad. After Baron Henry of Trutz-Drachen, ancestral foe of Otto's house, burns the castle in a raid and later severs Otto's right hand in retaliation for the murder of his kinsman by Otto's father, the two barons kill each other in a climactic purging of the old order of force and revenge. Otto, made a ward of the enlightened Emperor Rudolph, unites peaceful monastic values with the emperor's code of order and civility, restoring the fortunes of his house and marrying the daughter of his erstwhile enemy, his severed right hand replaced by a silver one emblematic of a new reign of peace and justice.

The polarity between civility and anarchy is clearly suggested in the novel's settings, the cold, dark robber Castles Drachenhausen and Trutz-Drachen contrasting with the Monastery of St. Michaelsburg and the emperor's bustling town of Nurnburg, centers of peace and prosperity. Called by Baron Conrad himself "a vile, rough place" (33), Castle Drachenhausen is surrounded by massive stone walls enclosing a bleak courtyard and "three great cheerless brick buildings, so forbidding that even the yellow sunlight could not light them into brightness" (4). Within is a cacophony of harsh sound, "the clash of armor, the ring of iron-shod hoofs, or the hoarse cry to arms" (28). The castle's watchtower, used to signal alarm and to summon the bandits to pillage, overlooks wild, impenetrable thickets and bare rocks where black swine feed "upon the refuse thrown out over the walls of the castle" (62). The castle chapel is now used only as a charnel and the worm-eaten old books belonging to its last, unremembered chaplain have long ago been lugged up to a loft to repose "among the mouldering things of the past" (61). This grim castle houses folk with "hard, rugged faces, seamed and weather-beaten" (59) and dominates "the wretched straw-thatched huts" and "vile hovels" of its dependent peasants, miserable serfs bound by chains of force and coercion to scratch out a meager subsistence while their wild, fierce children play "like foxes about their dens" (3–4).

The Monastery of St. Michaelsburg, on the other hand, nestles on a gentle slope swept with vineyards and crowned with fruitful "field and garden and orchard." Within its white walls, "where the warm yellow sunlight slept," all is peaceful quietness (27). The monastery bell tower summons the community to prayer and overlooks placid, cultivated vistas. A haven for gentle and prosperous scholars, husbandmen, farmers, and vintners, the monastery treasures priceless illuminated manuscripts featuring pictures of angels caroling to poor peasants, awarding them precedence over kings in their worship of the Christ Child. This pointed contrast between benighted castle and enlightened monastic community prepares for the eventual triumph of civility in Pyle's understanding of progressive medieval history. Just as St. Michael (patron of the monastery) triumphs in the battle for Heaven over the dragon (totem of Castle Drachenhausen), so the order and harmony fostered in the monastery and the emperor's court at Nurnburg will vanquish the brutal, anarchic sway of the lawless robber barons by novel's end.

These settings prepare the reader for the more significant contrast of deeds performed by the novel's central characters. Those associated with the monastery work toward a triumph over evil through suggestion and gentle persuasion, subtly, patiently in the face of numerous setbacks. The denizens of the castles, on the other hand, breed violence from violence, enmeshing themselves in a dense web of disaster, its deadly pattern woven from repeated cycles of outrage and reprisal unforgiven through generations. Baron Conrad, for example, recites a lamentable history to Abbot Otto while vowing revenge against his enemies: "their grandsire slew my father's grandsire; Baron Nicholas slew two of our kindred; and now this Baron Frederick gives me the foul wound and kills my dear wife through my body" (38). This legacy of woe leads to Conrad's cold-blooded murder of Baron Frederick, which in turn leads to Baron Henry's destruction of Castle Drachenhausen and mutilation of little Otto. The web of hatred and revenge grows so dense that at last both barons are enmeshed in it: coiled in each other's arms they drown together in a river, Baron Henry's retainers being so sated with the escalating violence that they at last decline to continue it after the death of their chief.

Such revenge and bloodshed are, however, ultimately not as durable as mercy and forgiveness, which transform violence and hatred into their opposites. Throughout the novel Otto, the embodiment of gentle kindness, remains physically the weakest character in Pyle's cast. Small and frail as a child, his quiet reserve leads many to think he is mentally deficient. Though conning his lessons quickly in the monastery, Otto gains the reputation even there of having "cracked-wits" like his mentor Brother John because their innocence and meek naiveté distinguish them from those in the world, much as does the "double-vision" of David and Hans Krout in *The Garden Behind the Moon* (1895), characters Otto and Brother John prefigure. As an adult, too, Otto is "powerless," his silver hand preventing him from ever drawing a sword or striking a blow, a beneficent consequence of his mutilation. Yet it is "weak" Otto who prevails over his stronger contemporaries by novel's end. Otto's influence for good is subtle but continuous, initiating the regeneration of his rough father and inducing One-Eyed Hans, his father's lieutenant, to spare a watchman during the rescue at Trutz-Drachen. Moreover, Otto ends the vicious cycles of retribution by begging Emperor Rudolph not to avenge him on the Trutz-Drachens but instead to allow him eventually to marry Pauline, daughter of his late enemy, the wisdom of which Rudolph concedes. Otto's later position in the emperor's court is one of quiet mediation, his words "listened to and weighed by those who were high in Council, and even by the Emperor himself" (169). Otto's new family motto—"A silver hand is better than an iron hand"—becomes the motto for the new age he helps the emperor to forge.

This image of the hand serves as a central unifying element in the novel, figuring, for example, in Brother John's vision of the Angel Gabriel whose hand, "as white as silver," grasps "a green bough with blossoms, like those that grow on the thorn bush" (45), an obvious emblem for Otto's own silver hand from which peace flows to begin the transformation of his harsh, thorny world into a blossoming garden. Later, Baron Conrad's desire that Otto "shall live as his sires have lived before him, holding to his rights by the power and might of his right hand" (53) is ironically frustrated by Baron Henry, who tells Otto that with his severed hand he will never "be able to strike such a blow as thy father gave to Baron Frederick" (95). This unifying image figures in several of the work's full-page illustrations as well, most notably in the prison scene at Trutz-Drachen where Otto instinctively cradles his right hand to his breast moments before Baron Henry severs it (93) and in the concluding illustration where Otto kisses, in reconciliation and love, the right hand of Pauline, daughter of his mutilator (171). This repeated image further unifies a plot already adroit in its contrasting interplay of violence and peace, its careful building of suspense through delayed revelations of thematically significant incidents, and its remarkable clarity and richness.

Indebted to Dürer and the German woodcut tradition—so much so that an admiring Joseph Pennell thought it "very hard to tell where Dürer ends and Howard Pyle begins"—the pen-and-ink illustrations feature a bold but intricate line, a wealth of articulated detail so ordered as to render the overall compositions dramatically spare and powerful.[8] These illustrations capture the thematic contrasts between the chaotic violence of the castle and the calm serenity of the monastery. Abbot Otto reading in his cell (29), for example, is an incarnation of quietude: the sand in the hourglass behind him seems barely to sift; his voluminous robes seem as monumental and immovable as the simple furniture of his cell; the man himself, intent upon his book, lives the interior and contemplative life of the mind. This stasis contrasts sharply with the following depiction of the wounding of Baron Conrad (35), the picture plane teeming with embroiled horses and men, their lances and swords arching in the background to complete the energetic swirl of the design. Across this circular composition cuts the strong diagonal lance of Baron Frederick to pierce Baron Conrad, prone at lower right, a dramatic and wholly successful focus on the illustration's central import against a superbly orchestrated backdrop of chaotic struggle. The following illustration marks a return to the quiet monastery (43), Brother John, his strange eyes wide open to his marvelous visions, holding Otto to his breast, the infant lulled into slumber by the droning of the hived bees in the background. These countering forces meet in the illustration depicting Otto's departure from the monastery (57), Brother John's simple, linear habit and innocent, open face at lower left contrasting with the convoluted figuration of the glinting chainmail worn by the scowling Baron and his men at upper right. Appropriately centered in the picture, Otto is destined to bridge the gap between these antithetical forces: he extends the charity and serenity of the monastery into the rough realm lying beyond monastic walls.

These full-page illustrations are complemented by a protocol of illuminated letters for each chapter, many with woodblock images from the *danse macabre,* and by tailpieces providing a central emblem for the chapters they close. In addition, chapter headpieces vie in beauty and fullness of conception with the full-page illustrations, within their small, carefully designed spaces distilling the essence of the chapters they introduce. The headpiece for the table of contents, for example, depicts a clarion angel heralding with trumpet the advent of peace, a branch of olive held in his right hand. The following headpiece for the foreword reveals the tenebrous nightmare world into which Otto is born, a world housing desperate peasants harried by the apocalyptic horsemen of unjust rule, war, and pestilence. Subsequent headpieces powerfully depict Death, hourglass in hand, tugging at the capes of the two barons before their fatal encounter (139, 149), and Emperor Rudolph seated in majesty, his right hand elevating a sword at which his nobles bow and his left hand dispensing a palm to a kneeling peasant (161). Behind him the clarion angel reappears, holding aloft a scale of justice. This headpiece summarizes the new order established at the conclusion of *Otto of the Silver Hand,* an order based essentially on the suppression of the "adventurer," that usually male character described by Paul Zweig as standing "outside the categories of duty and obliga-

"Poor Brother John Came Forward and Took the Boy's Hand"
Otto of the Silver Hand, 57

tion," as occupying an "unsocialized space" where, "self-derived" and "self-determined," he follows his inner destiny regardless of the claims made on him by home or community. In the course of the novel the "adventurers," epitomized by the willful barons, are swept away, to be replaced by Zweig's "hero," incarnated in the Emperor Rudolph and in Otto himself, each of whom is an exemplar of right behavior, protecting his society's values and "sacrificing his personal needs for those of the community."[9] *Otto of the Silver Hand* thus depicts the domestication of the hero, the welcomed triumph of rule and governance, of law and social order over unrestrained freedom and the heedless exercise of individual power. *Otto's* lawless robber-barons, however, swept by the river out to sea, emerge in subsequent reincarnations, often on pirate ships, to challenge again the rule of law in Pyle's later adventure romances.

Men of Iron (1892)

A historical novel like *Otto of the Silver Hand, Men of Iron* provides an accurate reconstruction of castle life in Henry IV's fifteenth-century England and sets into this precisely drawn, unromanticized portrait of the late Middle Ages a full complement of fictional characters and episodes. In *Otto of the Silver Hand* Pyle had been nearly as intent on chronicling the evolutionary progression in thirteenth-century Germany from lawless anarchy to social order as he was in delineating the fortunes of his main character. No such broad evolutionary social history informs *Men of Iron*. A bildungsroman, a more "private" history than that rendered in the earlier novel, *Men of Iron* features Myles Falworth's maturation to manhood, the channeling of his abundant energies toward socially constructive ends, and the eventual restoration of his family name and fortune through astute political maneuvering and Myles's skill at arms.

Roughly the first half of the novel, detailing Myles's childhood and youth, is modeled on *Tom Brown's Schooldays* (1857), the best-seller by Thomas Hughes, responsible for a host of contemporary "school-book" imitations. The novel's second half, chronicling Myles's progression from insouciant adolescence to responsible manhood, is the quintessential adventure story, replete with battles, narrow escapes, and a love affair eventually consummated through marriage after numerous obstacles. Through the four main parts of the story threads the measured unfolding of Myles's family history, the gradual revelation of injustice done, the identity of the perpetrator, and the righting of old wrongs.

The novel opens with a brief historical introduction chronicling the ascent of Henry IV over the dethroned Edward II, "weak, wicked, and treacherous," and the subsequent plot against the new king that plummets many, including the innocent Falworths, into disfavor and ruin.[10] The first chapter provides, with considerable psychological accuracy, the "bits and pieces" of the eight-year-old Myles's fragmented and impressionistic recollections of the murder before his eyes of Sir John Dale, a conspirator harbored briefly at Falworth Castle, and the later flight of the Falworths to sanctuary on the grounds of St. Mary's Priory, an oasis of peace similar to Otto's St. Michaelsburg. Myles's childhood there is an almost exact replica of Tom Brown's in the Vale of the White Horse: lads of indomitable pluck and mettle, Tom and Myles both play unselfconsciously with village boys of lower station, become adept at wrestling and the quarterstaff under the tutelage of grandfatherly household retainers, are introduced to the larger world at market-town fairs, and bid farewell to carefree childhood upon their departures for school.

The second section of the novel, detailing Myles's advent at Devlen Castle and his initial weeks there, continues this close imitation of *Tom Brown's Schooldays*. A fifteenth-century ancestor of the Browns, whom Hughes describes as "a fighting family," the pugnacious Myles battles his Flashman, Walter Blunt, no less than three times over the issue of fagging. Whereas Tom and his friend Scud East object, not to institutionally sanctioned fagging for the senior sixth-form boys, but to serving the fifth-form usurpers led by Flashman, the proud Myles objects to fagging in general, claiming that no shame "can be fouler than to do such menial service, saving for one's rightful Lord" (53). The "war of independence" waged by Tom Brown, East, and their cohorts, restricted to a few bedroom pranks against the older boys and an eventual refereed fistfight with Flashman, pales to a mere skirmish beside the quite serious campaign waged by Myles's "Knights of the Rose" against the senior bachelors led by Blunt. Myles doggedly pursues every opportunity to confront the enemy. In his first encounter with Blunt, the older boy nearly brains him with a thick wooden clog while the other bachelors hold him helpless on the floor. Myles's life is saved only by the timely intervention of Sir James Lee, supervisor of the castle squires. Myles's refusal to shake hands with Blunt soon leads to a second encounter where Myles is almost stabbed to death, though he manages, like Tom, to throw his enemy in a wrestling maneuver. Learning that Blunt and his henchmen lie in wait to slit his ears, Myles, dodging lethal cobbles, musters his "Knights" into combat with wooden staves, having been dissuaded by the castle smith from using "knives with blades a foot long, pointed and double-edged" (126). Finally, bleeding from the numerous injuries inflicted in a sword duel with Blunt, Myles manages to give his enemy a near-fatal head wound in a fight Pyle declines to detail, noting that combat "with a sharp-edged broadsword was not only brutal and debasing, but cruel and bloody as well" (135). In going further in his delineation of conflict and violence than even Hughes himself, whose paean to pugilism in *Tom Brown's Schooldays* is famous, Pyle strives for historical accuracy, his unsentimentalized picture of the Middle Ages being in many instances a dark one.

A psychologically complex character, the sixteen-year-old Myles is presented in this section of the novel as an honorable, attractive, but hypersensitive youth governed by hot-headed pride, quick to take offense and to come to blows. Admittedly, his foe, Walter Blunt, is a dangerous adversary indeed, unlike Flashman, who is merely annoying and nasty. But Myles is simply too avid for battle, extreme at times in seeking its occasions. This exaggerated pugnacity has its origins in Myles's natural propensity for action over debate as well as in his strong sense of alienation after learning from Sir James that his blind father is "an attainted outlaw" in great danger from a powerful foe (whom Myles intemperately declares he would kill on the spot). He also learns that the earl of Mackworth, in whose service he is enrolled, fears to come to his father's aid for political reasons. Thus Myles feels that he stands alone and must strike out at a host of enemies hedging him round. Sir James himself tells Myles that he can expect no open favor but must "live thine own life here and fight thine own way" (65). "I am friendless here," he later tells Sir James after his first encounter with Blunt, "and ye are all against me" (74). In thus showing the inner workings of his hero's mind, Pyle manages to maintain reader sympathy with a character prone to pride and violence, examples of which abound, leading Francis Gascoyne, Myles's Scud East, to chide him for constantly breeding trouble for himself and for being so foolish as "to come hither to this place, and then not submit to the ways thereof, as the rest of us do" (61).

Myles's head is filled with dangerous romantic claptrap and nearly homicidal notions of honor, a mind-set Pyle himself seems perilously close to admiring. For example, after Blunt has ignominiously clobbered him with the clog, Myles screams, "I will have his life that struck me when I was down!" (73), and later he founds the "Knights of the Rose," a crypto-Arthurian group dedicated to righting those wrongs in the castle that even Myles's closest associates must ask him to specify. At one point Myles uses as a pretext for conflict with the bachelors their beating of the lazy and exasperating Robin Ingoldsby, whose head Myles himself soon threatens to crack open with a block of wood. In short, though his resistance to tyranny is more often right than otherwise, Myles's bellicose behavior is unattractive, even if Sir James, "with a deal of dry gusto" (141), does describe to the delighted earl of Mackworth his multiple and near-fatal encounters as if they were mere boyish high jinks. Though seeming at times troubled by Myles's bloody strategies for ending fagging, a "tyranny" eventually to become the time-honored rule in Britain's great public schools, Pyle nevertheless admires his hero for his "savage bull-dog tenacity" (127) in winning his "first great fight in life" (141).

The transition from boyhood to adolescence in the novel's third section shows Myles as a juvenile rendition of the reckless and irresponsible adventurer, taken up as a protégé by the earl's brother, Lord George, a soldier of fortune. At this stage Myles manifests what Paul Zweig sees as a principal activity of the adventurer: he imparts marvelous tales of the unknown to those "destined to exist within the circle of domestic realities."[11] Myles's auditors are the earl's daughter and niece, the Ladies Anne and Alice, whom Myles visits at considerable risk seven times in their privy garden, a sanctuary so jealously guarded that previous interlopers have been shot with a crossbow or deprived of their ears. On these visits Myles tells of the dangerous and alien world of his "boyish escapades" to girls who "hear little of such matters" (158) until the earl puts a stop to the clandestine meetings. When Myles's chivalrous letter to his "sworn lady," Alice, is subsequently intercepted, the earl makes him realize his selfishness in compromising the girl, telling him he is now "old enough to have some of the thoughts of a man, and to lay aside those of a boy" (180), advice later echoed by Sir James when he informs Myles of the earl's friendship and presents him with a war horse. The earl thus plays the same role of adult male intercessor in Myles's development that Dr. Arnold plays in Tom Brown's.

By far the longest section of the novel is devoted to Myles's gradual transformation from adolescent to man, from adventurer to hero, a section filled with historical information about medieval knighthood and ceremony and resolving the tension threading throughout the work concerning Myles's adjustment of his family's position in the world and the identity of the family nemesis, the powerful earl of Alban. After his knighting by the king (whereupon he is proclaimed by all a reincarnation of Sir Galahad), his overcoming of the most renowned of the French champions in his maiden tilt, and a six-month stint in France with Lord George (where his tested virtue emerges wholly triumphant), Myles returns to London for the final showdown with Alban. A thoroughly conscienceless adventurer and thus the antithesis of the now-heroic Myles, Alban is the poisoned fount of all the Falworth troubles and the enemy of Mackworth as well. His climactic encounter with the young hero is invested with near-cosmic overtones: virtue versus vice; social responsibility versus selfish aggrandizement; honor and fair play versus malice and brutality. Myles's boyish avidity for violence has been so tamed that both before and after the battle he agonizes with Prior Edward over the ethics of killing an enemy like Alban in fair fight, obviously a difficult question for Pyle too, conditioned as he was by Quaker pacifism. Though the priest advises him that war and bloodshed, although cruel, are apparently placed in the world by God as an occasional means for bringing forth good from evil, Myles nevertheless spares Alban three times during their duel, a "false and foolish generosity," stemming from Myles's "impulsive youth" and his "romantic training in the artificial code of French chivalry" (317). The unchivalrous Alban does not reward this generosity, however, riding over Myles repeatedly when he is down, as he had done in the earlier blinding of Myles's father, and severely wounding him before being slain by Myles with a mace, the weapon Alban had murdered Sir John Dale with in the opening pages of the novel. *Men of Iron* culminates with the usual Pylean closure: the Falworth estates return to the family and Myles and the Lady Alice wed and live together happily, "for how else should the story end?" (329). *Men of Iron* thus supplies a model for maturation, much like those briefer ones Pyle would provide in the *enfances* of his Arthurian heroes. The novel assures its adolescent readers that if they have the necessary courage and pluck, they too, like Myles, can become "rich and happy and honored and beloved" after their "hard and noble fighting" (330). They can, in short, carve for themselves comfortable niches in the precarious adult world where they can live fruitful and productive lives.

The black-and-white halftone illustrations further suggest this thematic progression toward maturity. The pictures for the first three-quarters of the volume focus on Myles's dependence, isolation, and vulnerability, while those in the latter part show him in his full manhood, capable and independent. The first illustration after the frontispiece (28), for example, depicts Myles, small and alone in the foreground, kneeling to present his letter of petition to the powerful earl of Mackworth, who stands among his retainers. The illustration showing Myles held helpless on the ground, his head exposed to Blunt's murderous clog (70), reinforces the isolation and vulnerability of his early days at Devlen Castle. Other illustrations show him being called to account for his boyish actions by those older and wiser than himself (138, 170), and kneeling before King Henry to petition knighthood (216). Nowhere in the later illustrations is the adult Myles thus presented as vulnerable or suppliant. Instead, he stands forth boldly as an adult in his armor to receive Lady Alice's favor (250), walks in a newly attained equality with Prior Edward, his family benefactor (267), and resolutely denounces the earl of Alban before the king himself (308). Though thematically appropriate and often arrestingly composed and executed, the illustrations for *Men of Iron* do not share the imaginative pungency of Pyle's nimble pen-and-ink drawings, the reader's eye, according to Henry Pitz, traveling over these tipped-in gray halftone panels "without much temptation to linger and find long satisfactions."[12] No such criticism as the latter appends to the verbal text, however; *Men of Iron* remains one of Pyle's most popular books for adolescents.

Within the Capes (1885)

Published just two years after *Robin Hood*, *Within the Capes* establishes the pattern for many of Pyle's later adventure stories in its portrayal of a quiet Quaker jarred out of his pacific existence to face often violent adventures before returning to a calm and prosperous family life. The romance begins and ends with its octogenarian narrator's reflections on the two years during which more happened to him "than happens to most men in a lifetime," his adventures being a relatively brief interruption in a long life thoroughly "even and uneventful, excepting as to such small things as occur in [a] quiet Quaker neighborhood."[13]

The narrator, Tom Granger, recounts his adventures in the homely, artless, and digressive style appropriate for the ruminations of an old man. Hoping to preserve for posterity the story he has long been rehearsing orally, he writes to set the record straight, for he knows that things get so "monstrously twisted in passing from mouth to mouth" (2) that he fears being transformed over several generations into a posthumous pirate or murderer. Curiously, he writes of himself in third person, almost as if the young man whose early adventures he records is quite other than the garrulous, kindly old man whose life as a paterfamilias and pillar of his community is now drawing to a close. The "he" of his narrative is thus himself as other, outsider, an alien whose voyaging-out has placed him beyond the boundaries of the closed and landlocked society that eventually reclaims him after his adventuring days are done. This early alienation is a persistent theme in the novel. In the inland Quaker village of Eastcaster "little was known of the outside world" so that when Tom returns at novel's opening from a three-year cruise to the East Indies, he is looked upon "with a certain wariness, or shyness," his neighbors feeling "that he was not quite one of themselves" (26). Elihu Penrose is thus hesitant for Tom to marry his daughter, preferring that Patty choose someone "content to grow green in the same place that our fathers grew green before us" (31). When Tom returns a second time to Eastcaster after his later harrowing journey, he is thought to be "from foreign parts" (178), his long beard and graying hair so disguising him that even his closest friends fail to recognize him, believing him dead. An Ancient Mariner, he returns to hold his audience—Doctor White, his family, various neighbors, the reader—spellbound with the tale of his travels in the countries of the marvelous. Like Paul Zweig's archaic adventurers and ecstatic shamans, Tom Granger returns from the borders of death itself to name the unnameable for auditors stuck in conventional domestic routines; he "pushes back the essential ignorance" in which his neighbors live by "exposing a further reach of darkness to the clarity of words."[14]

As with most adventure tales, Tom's is essentially formulaic. Such formulas, according to Cawelti, "are at once highly ordered and conventional" though "permeated with the symbols of danger, uncertainty, violence and sex," allowing a reader to share in these "ultimate excitements," but in such a way that the reader's "basic sense of security and order is intensified rather than disrupted."[15] In other words, though formulaic literature often deals with the hazardous and chaotic, its familiar, predictable structures fulfill conventional expectations and thus confirm existing cultural views concerning the nature of reality and morality. *Within the Capes* is actually an amalgam of diverse popular genres, a conflation of the fictional formulas underlying the sentimental romance, the historical novel, the high seas adventure, the robinsonade, the buried treasure saga, the mystery and detective novel. The work of a young man, *Within the Capes* nevertheless evinces an authorial maturity in its careful pacing, controlled and unflagging action, appropriate narrative voice, and complete construction of setting and incident. The novel is a tour de force, an artfully composed inventory of formulaic conventions. In *Within the Capes* Pyle shows himself master of the many genres comprising the vast popular literature of the late nineteenth century.

The romance is almost pure action, its exciting plot assuming primacy over theme and character motivation. In the first chapters Pyle draws on the conventions of the sentimental romance to tell of Tom Granger's springtime return to Eastcaster, his falling in love with Patty Penrose at Quaker meeting, and the exaggerated emotional ecstasies and upheavals he experiences as a young man in love. This pastoral idyll, leisurely in its descriptions of woodland walks and innocent, tentative courtship, is interrupted by Elihu Penrose's demand that Tom show himself capable of supporting a wife on at least $750 a year, a demand that plunges Tom into the demonic realm of trial and adventure. Lured by the high pay, he takes a berth against his conscience in a Quaker privateersman, the *Nancy Hazlewood,* fitted out in Philadelphia to intercept British shipping for plunder during the War of 1812. Here Pyle's interest in American history leads to an account of British harbor blockades, the inadequate state of the American navy, and the common practice on both sides of legalized piracy. The blockade of the Delaware River temporarily lifted, the ship sets sail ten days before ready under a mysterious Captain Knight, who, it soon appears, is mentally unfit for his post, coming on deck wearing a broad red waist-scarf bulging with a brace of pistols while the doomed ship is foundering in heavy seas. Modeled on the popular sea epics of Captain Marryat and others, this absorbing high seas adventure involves a near-collision with a British man-of-war which looms out of a fog bank, a storm that causes the ill-prepared ship to founder, an insane captain who refuses to lower lifeboats or signal a rescue ship, and Tom's ensuing mutiny before the loss of the vessel, its copper hull rising higher and higher in Tom's subsequent nightmares as it sinks at the stern. Tom's archaic sense of honor remains intact through the crisis, Jack Baldwin, the first mate, having to tie him up and cast him into the lifeboat to prevent him from loyally perishing with the doomed crew. The ensuing lifeboat saga, anticipating Stephen Crane's "The Open Boat" (1898) by more than a decade, is an unsentimental chronicle of

weariness and privation, ending with the drowning in the surf of sev-
enteen crewmen, only Tom and Jack surviving to be cast up on a lonely
Caribbean island.

Pyle begins his subsequent robinsonade by attempting to differen-
tiate it from the many he has obviously read, having Tom claim that
"in real shipwreck," unlike fictional ones, "there is nothing either romantic or pleasant; neither is a desert island a cheerful place to dwell
upon" (115). But for the loneliness and Tom's yearning for Patty, however, this island is not so bad, the two castaways immediately settling
in to domesticate the wilds, much as Robinson Crusoe does in his
colonial venture of transforming his island into a little bit of old England. Thus Tom and Jack spend their time hollowing a cave home in
a sandhill, using the stoved-in lifeboat for a roof, and spending their
idle moments in constructing a raft and in writing rescue notes en-
closed in porpoise-skin bladders. One of these leads to their deliverance, but not before they feel the full effects of nature turned rabid in
the consummately described fury of the hurricane of 1814, perhaps the
eeriest and most evocative passage in the novel. The hurricane uncovers
a treasure from the wreck of a Spanish bullion ship, and Tom and Jack
leave the island wealthy men.

Just when it seems that Tom, having returned to Eastcaster, is set
for life, however, Pyle gives his already crowded narrative a final ad-
venturous twist. In any popular novel such as this one where plot is
primary, pure coincidence is almost always a regular feature. Thus,
Tom returns home on the eve of Patty's wedding to another man, who,
after a confrontation with Tom, is discovered murdered the next day.
From his prison cell Tom, with the help of the sloppy detective "Fatty"
Doyle, discovers the true murderer through a process of deduction and
ratiocination worthy of Conan Doyle's Sherlock Holmes, whose adventures first appeared in the 1890s. "Who would have thought," comments Will Gaines, Tom's Dr. Watson, "that such a quiet, dull-
seeming fellow as you, Tom Granger, would have thought out all this
for yourself!" (233–34). After the confession-suicide of the murderer,
Tom is free to marry Patty and rejoin the community from which he
has been alienated. He concludes his tale by comparing himself to a
ship, "one time battered and buffeted with the bitter storms of trouble
and despair, but now, full freighted with my cargo of years, safe at
anchor in my peaceful haven *Within the Capes*" (266).

This final metaphor suggests, however, that Tom's absorption into
the quiet Quaker community has perhaps not been as complete as he

repeatedly avows. Though landlocked for over half a century in seclud-
ed Eastcaster, he continues to think of himself as a voyager, spends
much of his time recounting (and vicariously reliving) his adventures,
marks the gatepost of his home with a chiseled ship under full sail,
and confesses to "a great longing" to revisit the scenes of his adventures, particularly the island of which he often dreams and now remem-
bers even more vividly than when the memory of it was fresh (116).
Indeed, the final act of his life is an imaginative re-creation of these
old adventures through his memoir, which paradoxically excludes any
details of his subsequent family life in Eastcaster, an indication, perhaps, that in spite of his disclaimers he considers those two years of
adventure to have been the center and focus of his existence. This subtle tension seems ironically to subvert the novel's indirect, though
dominant assertion—one which the narrator consistently affirms—that
home is best, that a steady life of labor and duty, of tending one's
garden, invariably leads to satisfaction and fulfillment.

The Rose of Paradise (1888)

In his first pirate book, *The Rose of Paradise* (serialized in *Harper's
Weekly,* 1887) Pyle recounts the history of Captain John Mackra's
bloody engagement in the Mozambique Channel with the infamous
Edward England and his pirate crew, adding "many lesser and more
detailed circumstances" to Charles Johnson's account in his standard
work on pirates, one of many volumes dealing with buccaneers and
corsairs in Pyle's personal library.[16] Using his source only as a point of
departure, Pyle invents an exciting plot revolving around England's
theft of an enormous ruby, the Rose of Paradise, and Mackra's successful strategy for recovering it. The narrative features the suspenseful
intrigues, violent clashes, narrow escapes, and providential coinci-
dences characteristic of the adventure romance, the conventions of
which Pyle had demonstrated mastery of in *Within the Capes.* Unlike
the earlier work, however, *The Rose of Paradise* combines fast action and
brute incident with skillful psychological portraiture, striking a balance between external event and internal character delineation.

This development in Pyle's adventure fiction corresponds with what
Paul Zweig sees as a post-Renaissance de-emphasis on external action
in the adventure story for an increasing interest in psychology or "the
exploration of interior space." Claiming that in modern romance "the
substance of adventure has been displaced inward," he argues that "the

framework of great exploits" has come to matter less than "the interior rhythm which the adventurer imposed upon the world of his experience."[17] Though *The Rose of Paradise* retains a full complement of "great exploits," it nevertheless manifests a new interest in internal motivation, Pyle's rounded characters being drawn with considerable psychological subtlety.

Its first-person narrator, Captain John Mackra, for example, is as careful to record his every feeling, reaction, and emotional state as he is to detail the actions that call forth these interior responses. The novel thus becomes as much a self-revelation as a tale of adventure, a chronicle of a mind under the stress of responsibility and duty, an intimate delineation of psychical nuance and coloration. All is transformed into matter for Mackra's self-reference and self-disclosure. Thus the naval conflict between Mackra and England becomes a counterpoint of external events and internal reflection, Mackra noting in the midst of battle, for instance, that this was the first time he had ever been under fire (83), seen a man killed in action (84), or observed the destructive force of a broadside (86). Witnessing these events, he chronicles all the shades of his "impatience and doubt and almost despair" (84). This swift interchange of outer impressions and the inner ones they evoke becomes the woof and warp of Mackra's chronicle. So intense at times is his introspection that he becomes an Odysseus adventuring on a dangerous sea of emotions, as when suspicion unjustly falls on him after the ruby is discovered missing. Striving to collect his thoughts "and to shape them into some sort of order," he is first possessed "with a most ungovernable fury," which gradually subsides into a strange calm. Before long, however, he becomes "consumed with anxiety" (174), this leading him into "the depths of gloomy despair" (176), from which he contemplates suicide before flinging himself on his knees in prayer, thereby recovering a certain peace of mind.

Mackra's internal disclosures do more than chart his inner voyagings, however. Taken in the aggregate, they provide an intimate psychological portrait of the hero of popular romance whose self-sacrifice and internal conquest of impulse and passion are as admirable as his extreme devotion to duty and his bravery in facing external trials. Throughout his narrative Mackra invariably shows himself to be modest, trusting, generous, resourceful, loyal, practical, and above all, selfless. Sacrificing his own needs for those of his community—according to Zweig a prime requisite for the hero—Mackra ventures his life to hold parley with the pirates, not so much in hopes of recovering the ruby and recouping his reputation as to secure the safety of his passengers and crew; he reasons that even if the pirates kill him, his death should satisfy their urge for revenge, thus deflecting their rancor from his shipmates. Later, though exiled and in disgrace himself, he finds England near death from a fever and nurses him, being so moved at finding the author of all his difficulties "prostrated, lying helpless, and deserted by all his kind" that he forgets his own troubles and thinks only of England's pitiable condition (213). Though Pyle shows Mackra to be a man above other men, he is careful not to turn him into a plaster saint. In his watch over England, Mackra later falls into an almost ungovernable rage at the sick man and must leave the hut to run "up and down, as one distracted" before being shown "what was right with more clearness" and resolving with difficulty not to desert "the poor and helpless wretch in his hour of need" (219). So imbued is Mackra with the primacy of duty and the necessity to live with honor that when all of his actions are misinterpreted by his superiors he feels he has nothing left to live for. Thus he tells the recovering England, who holds a pistol to his head, that since "I have lost my honor and all except my life through you . . . you might as well take that as the rest" (224). Indeed, so finely tuned is his honorable constitution that when he at last fathoms the full perfidy of Captain Leach, his passenger who first steals the ruby and then betrays the ship to the pirates, he feels a "great roaring" in his ears and a reeling of all things before fainting dead away (111). Again, when the board of inquiry at Bombay intimates its suspicions of him, he blanches and reels with vertigo, physically overcome (171).

No such delicacy disturbs the murderous pirate captain, Edward England, however. Deftly drawn, England is a Long John Silver, sharing with this antiheroic adventurer of Stevenson's *Treasure Island* (1883) a nature morally corrupt but nevertheless dangerously attractive because of his courage, intelligence, and occasional moral susceptibility. Though in nominal command of his pirate crew, he feels none of Mackra's fierce allegiance to them, knocking them about with blows and belaying pins; and they consequently feel none for him, eventually marooning him on the island of Mauritius where he is abandoned by all in his illness. The archetypal adventurer, England is an obvious foil for the heroic Mackra. Self-motivated and self-directed, he betrays the traitor Leach to his death and silently pockets the ruby for his personal enrichment. Yet, as in Captain Johnson's account, England's character is a chiaroscuro of good and evil. Though he will do nothing to endanger his own standing with the pirates, he nevertheless intercedes for Mackra on the pirate ship, and later, apparently recognizing Mackra's selflessness in nursing him, he grudgingly relinquishes the ruby. England's last act in the novel reveals his basic ambiguity, the retreating Mackra not being able to determine if the shot fired after him was meant to hurry him on or to murder him after a mercurial change of heart.

Certain of the minor characters, too, show this deftness of characterization, from the exasperatingly well-oiled and enterprising villain Leach to the popinjay Longways, whose humiliation at being posted as agent in such a bleak outpost as "King Coffee's" Juanna leads him into compensatory folly and self-importance. The delineation of the women characters, however, is not a success, they being given to fits of hysterical weeping and helpless hand-clasping. Mistress Pamela Boon, an imperiled Pauline, delivers her several lines in melodramatic, stilted tones and seems to be included in the work only to facilitate Pyle's usual matrimonial conclusion. The eight halftone illustrations, though excellently composed and executed, add little of substance to the tale's unfolding. Clearly, *The Rose of Paradise*, though plentifully leavened with action and suspense, is John Mackra's book. In the mannered but adept eighteenth-century style of his self-disclosure, Mackra reveals himself with an honesty, an ingenuousness, almost a naiveté that makes him one of the most engaging of Pyle's adventure heroes.

The Story of Jack Ballister's Fortunes (1895)

A lengthy historical adventure novel in fifty chapters, *Jack Ballister's Fortunes* offers a large cast of characters, an intricate plot, and a series of exciting adventures unfolding on two continents as well as on the high seas. Kidnapped from England and sold in Virginia as a "redemptioner" or indentured servant, Jack flees his brutal master to join Blackbeard's notorious pirates in North Carolina, later rescuing from them the captive heiress Eleanor Parker, whose grateful father champions Jack's rights to his inheritance in England. Pyle's most ambitious novel in this genre, *Jack Ballister's Fortunes* is a conflation of the formulas, themes, and fictional conventions used in his four previous adventure novels.

As in *Otto of the Silver Hand,* Pyle chooses as setting for this work a pivotal historical period in which order has not yet quelled anarchy, legality has yet to gain ascendancy over lawlessness. The early eighteenth-century American colonial period, as the introduction makes clear, was still characterized by a frontier morality, individual rights and the overarching sway of codified law not yet so firmly established as to prevent kidnapping or "man-stealing." In addition, pirates and buccaneers could still roam freely, often with the cooperation of colonial governments. The novel marks the end of such anarchy, chronicling the defeat of Blackbeard and his crew, that outlaw being "almost the last of the pirates who, with his banded men, was savage and powerful enough to come and go as he chose among the people whom he plundered."[18] *Jack Ballister's Fortunes* thus stems at least partially from Pyle's preoccupation with the nineteenth-century idea of progressive historical evolution, though the issue is not as central or as focused in this work as it is in *Otto of the Silver Hand.* Underlying both works, however, is a theme resonant with significance for Pyle's Anglo-American contemporaries then busily shouldering the "white man's burden," ostensibly to expedite the global replacement of barbarism with civility. By the conclusion of *Jack Ballister's Fortunes* Jack is able to marry Eleanor Parker and live a civilized life protected by law, apparently no longer having to fear that his children will be murdered by pirates, as his wife's brother had been, or spirited away for ransom, as had happened to Eleanor herself. Like Otto, Jack enters a new era at the end of his adventures.

More than a chronicle of broad social evolution, however, the novel also features Jack's individual maturation from reckless, willful adolescent to responsible adult, a theme underlying Pyle's earlier bildungsroman, *Men of Iron.* Jack's odyssey to manhood begins with his adoption at the age of sixteen by his unscrupulous and miserly uncle Hezekiah Tipton, who allows Jack "to go where he pleased and to do as he chose" (17), a harmful neglect resulting in Jack's living "an idle, aimless, useless life" (18). Thus ungoverned, Jack becomes selfish, disobedient, and manipulative, though his mean uncle deserves little better from him. Tipton's old housekeeper rightly complains, however, that Jack, always late for meals and tardy in performing the few chores she assigns him, thinks of nobody but himself (34). When Jack tries to extort twenty pounds from Tipton to buy a sailboat, threatening, if refused, to complain to his wealthy, aristocratic relative, Sir Henry

Ballister, Tipton sells him as an indentured servant to a Captain Butts, ironically receiving rather than parting with the twenty pounds Jack had demanded. On board the *Arundel* Jack is befriended by the reformed pirate Christian Dred, a grandfatherly mentor for the lonely adolescent then "passing from boyhood into manhood" (109). When Jack's willful idleness later reasserts itself at the home of his American master, he is threatened with a beating to teach him "to stay at home and 'tend to [his] own work" (147). Caught truant, Jack resists a horse-whipping and runs away, falling in with Blackbeard's pirates, the romantic accounts of their pillage and plunder so captivating his boyish imagination that he yearns to join them on their violent raids (241). Jack's regeneration begins, however, when the kidnapped Eleanor Parker tries unsuccessfully to flee her pirate captors. His sympathy for her sufferings leads to a growing sense of responsibility, the correction of his romantic, juvenile view of the pirates, and his eventual rejection of their anarchic way of life. Thus, his decision to rescue Eleanor represents a major step in Jack's maturation, his passage into adult heroism involving a hazardous chase during which his accomplice, Christian Dred, is killed, leaving him to save the girl on his own. Acclaimed a hero on his return, Jack experiences the awkward and inchoate yearnings of first love, journeys to England to claim his fortune and to receive a gentleman's education, and at last returns to Virginia to marry, always for Pyle an event marking the arrival of full maturity. Thus, the evolution Pyle saw occurring in eighteenth-century American colonial society finds its individual parallel in Jack Ballister's progression from adolescence to adulthood.

In constructing this narrative of social and individual maturation, Pyle drew upon a variety of popular fictional formulas, certain of which he had previously employed in *Within the Capes,* most notably the sentimental romance, the historical novel, and the pirate adventure tale. The work is, however, most clearly indebted to Robert Louis Stevenson's bestseller, *Kidnapped* (1886), especially in its opening episodes. *Jack Ballister's Fortunes* diverges from its predecessor in the abducted Jack's completed voyage to the American colonies, David Balfour's voyage to the same destination having been aborted by shipwreck off the cost of Scotland. Kidnapping is a repeated motif in Pyle's novel, Jack, Eleanor Parker, the lawyer Burton, Colonel Parker's servant Robin, and certain lesser characters all falling victim at some point to that crime. The story of Jack's adventures in the colonies following his kidnapping includes, interestingly enough, many of the conventions popularized in *Uncle Tom's Cabin* (1852) and in the ubiquitous nine-teenth-century American slave narratives, including Jack's desolation in captivity and his hard ocean crossing, his dehumanizing sale at the auction block, his life on an outlying plantation, and his running away from the ill-treatment of a brutal master. Underlying this slave narrative is the Cinderella tale of Jack's descent into servitude and the final revelation of his true identity and proper worth. Pyle skillfully weaves these disparate genres and conventions into a rich narrative tapestry highlighting the central pirate adventure tale.

As in *The Rose of Paradise*, the pirate adventure in *Jack Ballister's Fortunes* is an admixture of history and romance, Pyle adhering closely to his source in Captain Charles Johnson's standard history of piracy for the large outlines of Blackbeard's life and death. The novel provides intimate portrayals of pirate life and character, Blackbeard emerging as a surly and unpredictable adventurer, congenitally incapable of living the quiet, domestic life he pledges himself to in accepting the king's pardon. No cardboard villain, Pyle's Blackbeard is brave and self-pos-sessed, daring, resourceful, and articulate, a humanized version of the historical figure who by Pyle's time had become obscured in a dark halo of lurid legend. The Blackbeard in this work is a man, albeit wicked, and not the exaggerated demon incarnate depicted in popular histories as going about with plaited beard, blackened face, and flam-ing hempen punks thrust under his hat brim. Richard Parker, Black-beard's collaborator in the abduction of Eleanor, on the other hand, is a stock character, a spoiled younger son given to cards and cockfight-ing, a handsome, well-educated cad who has frittered away his inher-itance. Of the novel's villains, however, only Christian Dred, as his name implies, approaches the complexity of Stevenson's Long John Sil-ver and Pyle's Ned England, all three scoundrels admitting to mo-ments of moral susceptibility. Dred is certainly villainous enough: he masterminds many of Blackbeard's raids, betrays his pardon by return-ing to piracy, and murders Eleanor's brother during an attack on a ship. But at the same time he is inherently, ironically kind, befriending Jack on his voyage to the colonies, offering protection to him when he runs away from his master, and sacrificing his life to rescue Eleanor in pro-pitiation for his earlier murder of her brother. Dred and Jack are clearly the most complex characters in the novel. Lieutenant Maynard and Eleanor's father, Colonel Parker, are one-dimensional heroic figures, and Eleanor herself is an exasperatingly passive ingenue.

The black-and-white oil illustrations for the work resemble in rep-

"Mr. Parker Stood Looking Steadily at His Visitor"
The Story of Jack Ballister's Fortunes, facing 122

resentational style those for *The Garden Behind the Moon,* their strong
visual designs reinforcing the semantic intentions of the text. In Pyle's
depiction of the meeting of Blackbeard and Richard Parker to plot
Eleanor's abduction, for example, each of the villains casts a huge,
menacing shadow, their dark coronas of malice eventually blighting
the happiness of many innocent people (122). In the portrayal of Jack's
first significant encounter with Eleanor, by contrast, Pyle suggests a
world of innocence and light by eliminating all shadows, though Jack
seems tentative and ill at ease before Eleanor, self-assured and at home
in her father's grand house (132). The concluding illustration depicts
Jack and Eleanor, now young adults with their trials borne, standing
on a terrace and looking out on a world newly opened to them (408).
Thus, the novel concludes with the return of its central characters to
normal, orderly lives after their exciting, often terrifying adventures in
the demonic realm, a coda similarly employed in the four preceding
historical adventure novels from which this work draws its themes and
borrows many of its fictional conventions.

Stolen Treasure (1907); *Howard Pyle's Book of Pirates* (1921); *The Ruby of Kishmoor* (1908)

Jack Ballister's Fortunes, the last and longest of Pyle's full-length adventure novels, is succeeded by relatively short pirate fiction written for the magazines and by a culminating parody of the pirate adventure genre.

In the introduction to his 1891 edition of John Esquemeling's *Buccaneers and Marooners of America* Pyle provides an apologia for his avid interest in pirate adventure, arguing that pirate tales fascinate because beneath "the accumulated *debris* of culture" there exists a "hidden ground-work of the old-time savage" ever receptive to deeds fierce, violent, and lawless.[19] This "nether man that lies within us" (16), unsubdued by the veneer of culture, instinctively hungers for "constant alertness, constant danger, constant escape," for "blood and lust and flame and rapine," a hunger safely, if temporarily, appeased by pirate tales that give voice to our deep discontents with civilization and serve as conduits for the venting of a "hell of unbridled passions let loose to rend and tear" (17). Thus, according to Pyle, the pirate's "courage and daring, no matter how mad and ungodly, have always a redundancy of *vim* and life to recommend them" to the unregenerate creature raging in each of us (16). No less important, pirate tales satisfy our lust for wealth, the fancy reveling as much in sudden, often unscrupulous acquisitions of huge fortunes as in the courage and daring necessary to win them. And for the more intellectually inclined, pirate adventure allows valuable insights into "a mad, savage, unkempt phase of humanity" (25), the history of piracy being a cautionary "verisemblance of the degeneration, the quick disintegration of humanity the moment that the laws of God and man are lifted" (38). History, for Pyle, is always a two-way street: on the one hand, it chronicles a progressive social evolution (as charted in *Otto of the Silver Hand* and *Jack Ballister's Fortunes*), and on the other, a regressive deterioration, a devolution (as in Pyle's account in the introduction to Esquemeling of the descent from officially chartered privateersman to buccaneer to marooner). Ever the didact, Pyle thus believed that there was "a profitable lesson to be learned in the history of such a human extreme of evil" as piracy, that wicked "rebound from civilization" (39). In addition, he saw pirate romance as a safety valve or escape hatch for civilized human beings: it satisfied in a socially acceptable way the primal, amoral human urge

to lawless adventure at the same time that it reinforced the laws insti-
tuted to curb that urge.

Pyle's magazine pirate stories, miniaturizations of his longer pirate
novels, usually feature the adventures of a young male hero, on the
whole brave, good, honest, and dutiful, who shares, willingly or otherwise, certain lawless escapades with a courageous but conscienceless
pirate adventurer before returning to the security of the domestic realm
to uphold in his career and inevitable marriage the laws and restraints
of his society. This hiatus in the young hero's otherwise orderly life is
invariably described in the stories as a dream or nightmare, a descent
into the demonic realm from which the hero eventually awakens. The
formula for Pyle's pirate adventures, replete with incidents of anarchy
and chaos, grants a reader vicarious participation in antisocial dangers,
violence, and crime at the same time that it formally affirms societal
values through its highly ordered and predictable structure. Pirate adventure thus provides its readers with a medium whereby they can
imaginatively experience courageous lawlessness at the same time that
they can reject it.

Of the four pirate stories by Pyle collected in *Stolen Treasure,* the
first, "With the Buccaneers" (*Harper's Round Table,* June 1897), embodies this plot formula in the most spirited and straightforward way.
Young Harry Mostyn escapes in 1665 from his large, prosperous family
of sugar planters to join the pirate Henry Morgan, who promises to
make a man of him. Under Morgan's tutelage, Harry witnesses cold-
blooded murder, participates in the amazing capture of a heavily armed
and manned Spanish flagship, is involved in a naval battle during
which he risks death to save Morgan's ship, and engages in a dalliance
with an exotic French girl before being peremptorily reclaimed by an
older brother and then settling down as "a respectable and wealthy
sugar merchant with an English wife and a fine family of children."[20]
Harry's adventures amount to little more than a boisterous lark, a
dreamlike interstice between periods of adherence to the approved social pattern affirmed by the story's end.

The three subsequent works in the collection offer variations and
elaborations on this basic formula. In these works Pyle often relied
upon incredible coincidence to mold his narrative structures into pleas-
ing but highly improbable geometrical plot designs. The order of
placement of the four stories in *Stolen Treasure* is thus determined, not
by chronological publishing dates, but by increasingly daring variations on the formula underlying them all. In "Tom Chist and the Trea-

sure-Box" (*Harper's Round Table*, March 1896), for example, Pyle makes his hero a foundling whose adventures culminate in the contrived but nevertheless satisfying revelation of his proper identity and high social position. One night observing Captain Kidd burying treasure by moonlight, Tom soon retraces the pirate's steps and acquires the fortune for himself, later journeying to consult Richard Chillingsworth, one of the wealthiest, most influential men in New York, about some papers found in the chest. In one of several plot contrivances straight from nineteenth-century melodrama, Tom suddenly discovers that Chillingsworth is none other than his uncle, whereupon he marries Chillingsworth's daughter and becomes "rich and great" (94), assuming his full position as a staunch upholder of mainstream values while Kidd continues to subvert them until his last frolic on the gallows. A similar quilt of coincidence and predictable formulaic patterning, "The Ghost of Captain Brand" (*Harper's Weekly*, 19 December 1896), the third work in the collection, details the adventures of Barnaby True, whose grandfather, the notorious pirate William Brand, had been assassinated by his protégé Jack Malyoe twenty years before the story begins. In Jamaica on business, Barnaby joins with Abram Dowling, a former associate of his grandfather, to avenge the murder and to secure the treasure. In an ensuing battle Malyoe suffers a fatal stroke after seeing the ghostly apparition of Captain Brand, who appears again later in the flashes of lightning of a storm off Staten Island on the eve of Barnaby's marriage to Malyoe's niece, Marjorie. One of the most interesting of the magazine pirate stories, "Captain Brand" introduces into the formula an ambiguity similar to that underlying Henry James's *The Turn of the Screw* (1898), the reader being unable to determine if Captain Brand is indeed dead and returns as a ghost, or if, alive, he has for twenty years been directing events to this conclusion, evidence for both interpretations being carefully planted in the text.

Another tale of the quasi-supernatural, this one with a rational explanation, "The Devil at New Hope" (*Harper's Weekly*, 18 December 1897), involves the return of the pirate and slave trader Obadiah Belford to New Hope to torment his respectable but pompous brother William. Reputed to be in league with the devil, Obadiah maliciously engineers the ruinous marriage of his brother's only child to a man he believes to be a runaway servant, or worse, but whom he presents as the second son of an earl. Possible only in popular formula fiction, Obadiah's impostor turns out to be the real thing, this irresponsible young aristocrat becoming so revolted by Obadiah's depravity that he returns to the paths of righteousness, following them with his wife all the way to an eventual peerage.

Certainly Pyle knew that the stories in *Stolen Treasure* were not great literature. Well-crafted and engagingly written potboilers, they provide vicarious adventure, exciting escape, wish fulfillment, a comforting predictability, and a confirmation of traditional values. They also furnish insights into turn-of-the-century popular literary taste, a taste apparently persisting well into the twentieth century, as is evidenced by the 1949 reissue of *Howard Pyle's Book of Pirates*, originally published in 1921. A posthumous compilation of pictures and prose selections from Pyle's pirate works, the *Book of Pirates* also reprints two interesting magazine stories, both "Blueskin the Pirate" (1890) and "Captain Scarfield" (1900) centering on the usual Pylean conflict between the sedate, civilized man of law and his alter ego, the lawless adventurer.[21] In "Blueskin the Pirate," as in "The Devil at New Hope," the combatants are brothers, but in "Captain Scarfield" the conflict becomes internal, the central character being both a prominent, devoutly pacifist Quaker and a notably bloodthirsty pirate, as Captain Cooper a paragon of business integrity and domestic regularity in Philadelphia and as Captain Scarfield a murderous sea robber and keeper of a mulatto wife in the West Indies. Clearly influenced by Stevenson's *Dr. Jekyll and Mr. Hyde* (1886), this short work offers a portrait of a man in whom "the separate entities of good and bad each had, in its turn, a perfect and distinct existence" (206). Indeed, Pyle posits Cooper/Scarfield as an emblem for civilized man: "Who," he asks, "within his inner consciousness, does not feel that same ferine, savage man struggling against the stern, adamantine bonds of morality and decorum? Were those bonds burst asunder, as it was with [Scarfield], might not the wild beast rush forth, as it had rushed forth in him, to rend and to tear?" (206-7). More than just a fictional embodiment of Pyle's historical, psychological, and anthropological theories of human nature, however, "Captain Scarfield" is also a classic Pylean adventure tale, complete with a dashing young hero, Lieutenant Mainwaring, who brings to an end Scarfield's depredations in the West Indies and eventually marries the pirate's wealthy young niece.

In these magazine stories Pyle explored the fictional possibilities of the popular pirate adventure genre he chose to work in, creating numerous variations on a common underlying formula and theme. In *The Ruby of Kishmoor* (1908; *Harper's Monthly,* August 1907) he demonstrates his complete command of this genre and bids farewell to it in a parody, much as he had earlier parodied the conventions of the sentimental romance in *The Price of Blood*. A slight and sensational tale, *The Ruby of Kishmoor* opens with a prologue recounting Captain Keitt's pirate theft of a great ruby, his subsequent murder, and the deaths of all but three of his original crew. This background established, the tale introduces Jonathan Rugg, a Philadelphia Quaker under whose "sedate and sober demeanor" lie hidden the most romantic aspirations for adventure and "unwonted excitement."[22] On his first night in Jamaica, which Rugg finds an "extraordinary land of enchantment and unreality" (11), a mysterious veiled woman entrusts to his safekeeping a small ivory orb. First a little gentleman with one eye, then a foreigner with silver earrings, and finally a sea captain with a flattened nose try to murder Rugg on being shown this bauble, each of them being killed instead in their struggles with the astonished Quaker. The tale concludes with a horrified Rugg returning the ivory ball to the woman, who then identifies herself as the daughter of Captain Keitt and explains that she has been menaced by three treacherous pirates who had previously killed her father in order to acquire the fabulous Ruby of Kishmoor hidden in the ivory container. When she offers Rugg her ruby, her wealth, and her hand, he refuses all in alarm and hurries back to Pennsylvania to marry plain Martha Dobbs and to content himself "with such excitement as his mercantile profession and his extremely peaceful existence might afford" (73). The sale of a rope of pearls arriving mysteriously on his wedding day transforms him into one of the "leading merchants of his native town of Philadelphia" (74).

Pyle conceived of the tale as a joke, its humor emerging from the ironic contrast between Rugg's dogged Quaker earnestness and the extravagantly romantic adventures befalling him, their near-hallucinatory quality emphasized by Pyle's impressionistic portraits and vignettes in colored oils, which start out from their dark backgrounds as if suddenly illuminated by a flare. As in Pyle's other pirate stories and novels, the hero of *The Ruby of Kishmoor* yearns for adventure and escape, experiences it, and then returns to the security of the domestic realm. But Jonathan Rugg is anything but heroic, his feats being accomplished by accident rather than by skill or intention. The villains seem more like the Marx Brothers than bloodthirsty cutthroats, and the exotic Evaline Keitt is little more than a nineteeth-century music-hall houri. In this parody of the pirate-tale formula Pyle bids farewell to his earlier, more serious pirate works, most notably *Within the Capes* (with its confrontation of quiet Quaker with boisterous adventure) and

The Rose of Paradise (with its focus on a magnificent stolen ruby hidden in a cocoon of yarn). A fast-paced, perfectly plotted, amusing burlesque, *The Ruby of Kishmoor* is an appropriate conclusion to Pyle's long fascination with the pirate adventure story.

Rejected of Men (1903)

In a 17 May 1891 letter William Dean Howells acknowledged receipt of an unfinished essay by Pyle on "immortality and infinity," commended him on the cogency of his speculative thought, and suggested that such abstruse subjects would appeal to a broader audience if they were "somehow dramatically presented" rather than abstractly dissected into "propositions and conclusions."[23] Pyle followed this advice in *Rejected of Men*, a philosophical novel highly praised by Howells for both content and method of presentation and featuring what Pyle himself termed his "radical opinions" concerning free will and divine providence, reason and faith, the divergent ways of God and man, and the gulf between rich and poor in the American class system. Though frequently revised and rewritten over a period of nine years, *Rejected of Men* does not succeed well as a novel, its abstract intellectual framework only incompletely camouflaged by a thin fictional overlay. Intended as a "realist" work in the Howellsian vein, the novel remains primarily a philosophical disquisition, its multiple "messages" assuming primacy over action, plot, and story. Even the portrayal of character and setting, the latter generally one of Pyle's strengths, remains superficial and sketchy rather than penetrating, curiously flat and two-dimensional in spite of occasional careful delineation and adroit "social realist" description, especially of the impoverished environment in which Christ and his disciples operate. *Rejected of Men* reveals Pyle's surprisingly radical theological speculations, partially drawn from his reading of Swedenborg, at the same time that it affirms his faith in Christianity, the novel's New Testament sequence and structure providing a traditional narrative frame for his religious unorthodoxy.

Rejected of Men delineates Christ's ministry and death as translated "from the ancient Hebrew habits of life into modern American."[24] Interesting for its Jamesian experiments with point of view, the novel is narrated by a late nineteenth-century New York "Pharisee" who presents his perspective on "the great events of sacred history" in order to vindicate the actions of his class in condemning Christ to death (vi). Noting that the Gospel accounts present Christ as the central figure around whom all men revolve, this narrator provides a reverse point of view, the perspective of the scribes, Pharisees, Levites, and certain Romans for whom Christ was neither dominant nor pivotal but merely a single integer in a large, complex society. This alternate perspective thrusts Pilate, Herod, Caiaphas, and the rich young man into the foreground, the novel's focal center, while Christ and his unsavory followers are transformed into dimly glimpsed and marginal figures operating in the background. In thus reversing the perspective informing the Christian Gospels, the narrator establishes the inevitability of Christ's condemnation by those scribes and Pharisees identified with the social and moral order challenged by the Messiah and his disciples.

As the narrator repeatedly avows, Christ is executed because he threatens the status quo. The reverse of *Otto of the Silver Hand,* which depicts a lawless and anarchic society groping toward order and legality, *Rejected of Men* portrays the decadence that can beset an established order incapable of change or regeneration, one which suppresses dissent and nonconformity and maintains an unjust division between the rich and the poor. In *Otto* and *Men of Iron*, in the pirate adventures as well, Pyle showed the undesirable consequences of renegade behavior and the necessity to curb "the nether man" through moral check and social restraint. In *Rejected of Men*, however, the social and moral order has grown so rigid as to be perpetuated for its own sake and not for the safeguarding of the rights of all. In depicting a social order ripe for revolution because contributing to the comfort and security only of the "Gilded Age" rich and powerful, the novel explores yet another aspect of the persistent dialectic in Pyle's fiction between chaos and order, license and law.

So profound is the disparity between rich and poor in the novel's version of late nineteenth-century America that the two classes cannot even speak to each other, a point made repeatedly by the narrator and by various characters in the novel, including Bishop Caiaphas, his son-in-law the rich young man Henry Gilderman, and his lawyer, Judah Inkerman, who notes that the poor "neither think nor feel" as do the rich, nor do they have "the same sort of logical or moral ballast to keep them steady" (233). While the rich buy Rembrandts, rare books, and fine horses, build fancy houses, attend posh parties, dine at club, and lose small fortunes at cards and the races, the poor labor and in their off-hours traipse about the countryside after itinerant preachers like the Baptist and Christ himself. On the evening that Christ undergoes his agony and arrest in the public park, Gilderman attends an extravagant anniversary party and later wins several thousand dollars at poker. Thus, concludes the narrator, a gulf, "not wide but as profound as infinity, separates the rich man from the poor man, and there is no earthly means of crossing it" (235). Certainly no bridge is constructed during the course of the novel. A pervading sense of fatalistic futility thus permeates the work, stemming not solely from the hopelessness of class relations but also from the apparent inability of the novel's fated characters to exercise any free will or moral choice. Part of the Pharisee narrator's exculpation of his class for Christ's murder, for example, originates in his belief that all must "fulfill the destiny that Providence has assigned": "If we were made virtuous," he contends, "we must under normal conditions be virtuous; if we were made vicious we must be vicious; and there the matter ends" (viii). This pervading fatalism seems more than a meretricious excuse invented by the narrator to escape culpability, however. The actions of Bishop Caiaphas, too, seem predetermined, as do those of Henry Gilderman, described as locked by his enormous wealth "into a shell of circumstances from which there is no escape" (63–64).

Almost as dispiriting as this sense of fatalism in the novel is the narrator's seeming pessimism concerning the ability of nearly all but the reeking, ragged, and uneducated poor to place themselves in a proper relationship with God. In his "interludes" the Pharisee twice halts the narrative progression to deliver himself of abstract metaphysical tracts, one concerning the necessity for most people to substitute a white-robed, visionary spirit for the inconvenient flesh-and-blood reality of Christ and the second concerning the universal propensity to worship a humanly created image of God rather than God himself. These tendencies stem from the frequently noted divergence between the ways of God and man, for God "does not shape His events as we would have them shaped; He shapes them exactly different" (204), making it difficult indeed for most to understand, let alone accept, God's will. As the narrator remarks concerning his initial rejection of the teachings of the uncouth Baptist, "it cannot be possible that [God] expects us, scribes and pharisees, whom He has endowed with intelligence and reason, to accept that which was so unintelligent and so unreasonable" (41). The novel's theological pessimism climaxes in the inability of Gilderman, a sensitive, honest, sincere man, to follow Christ's radical command to give up everything in exchange for eternal life. "God have mercy on us all!" the narrator prays, for in Christ's "dreadful" command "lies the secret of heaven and of earth and of all that is and of all that is to come, and yet not one of us dares to open the gates of heavenly happiness. The world seems so near and that other supreme good so very remote" (181).

Contrary to Pyle's expectations, *Rejected of Men* did not cause any great literary stir or controversy when, after numerous rejections, it was finally published by Harper's in 1903. Though the novel has some fine passages, most notably the eerie, dispassionate account of the raising of Lazarus, it nevertheless fails as both fiction and philosophical text. Wooden and unattractive characters, cardboard settings by and large, and a plot lacking in tension or particular interest damage the work as a novel, and its "realist" manner seems uncongenial to a writer notable for his romances. In addition, the philosophical/theological ideas, resonant with sincerity and an almost painful earnestness, do little to establish Pyle as an original thinker, though they convincingly demonstrate the difficulties of being a Christian in the modern world. Pyle himself seemed to recognize the incongruity of *Rejected of Men* in his oeuvre. In a letter to his publisher about the work he aptly compared himself to a light comedian who suddenly startles his audience with a serious discussion of the tragic aspects of life.[25] *Rejected of Men* was a brief, dead-end departure from the lively adolescent and children's fiction on which Pyle's literary reputation mainly rests.

Chapter Five
The Achievement of Howard Pyle

Howard Pyle's career was characterized by a remarkable synthesis of his talents as writer, illustrator, and teacher. In all three areas he excelled, and at the time of his death in November 1911, his books for children were still in popular demand, his illustrations and paintings were attracting thousands of viewers to a retrospective exhibit held in Wilmington in March 1912, and the works of his many students were to be seen in all of the leading American illustrated periodicals. Though Pyle's popular reputation has declined over the intervening years, even now his works for children are still in print in multiple editions, his illustrations and canvases command high prices in the marketplace, and the "Brandywine Tradition" initiated by Pyle and continued by his many pupils remains a force in contemporary American art. Pyle's current reputation, however, rests primarily on his historical importance. He is now recognized as a classic American writer for young people, a significant figure in what has come to be called "the first Golden Age of Children's Literature." In addition, he is remembered as one of the most influential educators in the history of American art, and is frequently referred to as the "Father of American Illustration" for his seminal role in elevating American illustration to a position of world eminence.

Pyle's artistic career, admirably assessed in Henry C. Pitz's 1965 study, paralleled the rise of the great American periodicals and the increasing public demand after the Civil War for visual accompaniments to the printed word.[1] In meeting this demand, Pyle dedicated himself to transforming book and magazine illustration, up to then often considered mere hackwork, into a recognized branch of the fine arts. In addition, he set out to form an indigenous American school of illustration free of what he felt to be a slavish dependence on European models and techniques. Through the example of his own works and through his many pupils, Pyle came to exercise a dominant influence on the illustration of his day and after. Thus, according to N. C.

Wyeth, Pyle was largely responsible for the brilliant emergence of American magazine and book illustration from that "slackwater period" which "came at the end of the Victorian era—a period singularly stagnant in the field of graphic expression."[2]

Pyle's career spanned almost all of the major early technological advances in American printing and reproduction. Since he was eager to exploit the opportunities offered by each new technical advance, the aggregate of his illustrations offers a capsulized history of the rapid innovations in American reproduction at the turn of the century. His early drawings, for example, had to be painstakingly transferred onto woodblocks by skilled engravers, a time-consuming process little changed from the days of Dürer, one of the chief influences on Pyle's visual style. Soon, however, Pyle was illustrating in black-and-white oils for halftone reproduction, a new photoengraving process. Though early attempts to reproduce his illustrations in color were often less than technically successful, his 1900 Harper illustrations for Erik Bogh's "The Pilgrimage of Truth" were a triumph from which dated the rapid perfecting of American color reproduction processes.

Of the thousands of illustrations produced during an amazingly prolific career, Pyle's black-and-white pen drawings best stand the test of time. N. C. Wyeth's 1925 assertion that these drawings vie "with the greatest works of all time done in this medium" is, even today, neither eccentric nor particularly inflated.[3] The *Robin Hood* illustrations, as well as those for the fairy-tale collections, *Otto of the Silver Hand*, and the Arthur books, continue to claim an enduring place in the pictorial imagination and represent Pyle's most important contributions to American art. Wyeth's summary assessment that these drawings represent Pyle's "highest artistic achievement" represents current critical judgment.[4] In the 10 May 1972 *New York Times Book Review*, for example, Hayward Cirker, president of Dover Publications, admitted that he reissued Pyle's best works for juveniles, not for the texts, but because their line drawings are so "magnificent"; and John Rowe Townsend, no advocate of Pyle's prose, accords him high praise for his pictorial designs, calling him "the outstanding late-nineteenth-century American" illustrator in a field dominated by luminaries.[5]

Pyle's historical illustrations and paintings, so numerous as to compose a pictorial early history of the nation, still resonate in the American consciousness, for from them we derive many of our images of the colonial and Revolutionary War periods. Though we may no longer attribute these images directly to Pyle, they have become embedded in our pictorial memories. His passion for historical accuracy, his astute distillation of the significant historical moment, and his collaborations with such eminent historians and statesmen as Woodrow Wilson and Henry Cabot Lodge shaped for his contemporaries, and in a more submerged fashion for posterity, a prevailing vision of early American costume, character, and event. On the other hand, Pyle's adroit medieval and pirate pictures, so highly praised in his day and soon after, no longer command significant attention, primarily because their subjects have so completely gone out of vogue.

Howard Pyle produced his best illustrations for his children's works, and as a writer for children his reputation remains secure. A new climate in literary and pictorial taste in juvenile entertainments has, however, done much to diminish the popular demand for his children's works that he enjoyed during his lifetime. Complex and dense in verbal style and visual design, prone to didacticism and laden with deliberate archaisms, Pyle's works do not compete well with the instantaneous, often crudely immediate images and plots featured in contemporary comic books, many recent picture books, popular movies such as *Star Wars*, and Saturday morning cartoons. Nevertheless, his classic works for children continue to delight sophisticated child and adult readers alike and still claim an enthusiastic audience, however diminished. His works for children live and breathe even in our smoggy air because they evince a masterfully created idyllic realm, a golden time-out-of-time, a pastoral oasis, the innocence and robust freshness of which still propel the contemporary reader through the borders of Arcadia. This "Land of Fancy," variously named "Wonderland," "Never-never-land," and "Twilight Land," this safe refuge of "jollity and mirth," is no saccharine commonwealth, sticky with sugarplums and cushioned with gumdrops. Nor is it a darkly romantic country rigged up with operatic stage sets, dreamy and vague, glimmering with watery moonlight and replete with moldering castles and crumbling towers, that overstuffed furniture crowding the works of so many nineteenth-century romantic imitators of Tennyson and the Rossettis. Instead, Pyle's Arcadia is sun-drenched, invigorating, and fragrant; its habitations airy, spacious, clean-swept, and lived-in; its citizens robust and exuberant, above all muscular and alive, endowed with a delight and youthful wonder at the ample proportions of the land they occupy and at the fullness of creation in general. Pyle's "Land of Fancy" is ultimately so endearing, however, because it is paradoxically so unstable, so fleeting, threatened on every side by death, disillusion, and the passage of time. These verities are heroically held in abeyance in Pyle's pastoral idyll, fended off for a hearteningly long period, but they cannot be dispelled forever. Thus Robin Hood, after sporting long in his greenwood "Land of Fancy," loses his idealism and declines toward death. Thus, too, the grassy oasis in *Pepper & Salt* dissolves to the quotidian duration of schoolwork and chores, and the Wonder Clock ceases its hypnotic ticking so that Father Time stirs from his revery to retrieve his scyth and hourglass. Twilight Land fades to darkness, the roses of the Moon-Garden blanche and wither, and Arthur, too, for so long resplendent in breezy Camelot, sinks to grief. Pyle's "Land of Fancy," then, is a land bordered by loss, a glorious golden fabric frayed at its edges. His achievement and the continuing vitality of his works for children lie in his ability to suspend momentarily the depredations of time, to prolong and heighten that marvelous interval wherein youthful wonder and mirth exist untarnished.

These works for juveniles are historically important in the evolution of American children's literature. Pyle was instrumental in the nineteenth-century revitalization of the folktale, the conventions of which are everywhere to be found in his works and culminate in a series of vivid and highly entertaining fairy tales. His folktale collections and his Robin Hood and Arthur series mark a significant break with Victorian stiffness and formality in their defense of merriment and light-heartedness over ponderous morality, starched primness, and grim utilitarianism. In preface after preface Pyle defends the "innocent jollity and mirth" to be found in the pages of his volumes, offering "a pinch of seasoning in this dull, heavy life of ours," a momentary respite for those who "plod amid serious things." These prefaces pointedly exclude from his audience such dour Victorians as *Pepper & Salt*'s "sober wise man" and all those even now "who think that life hath nought to do with innocent laughter that can harm no one."[6] In seeking to dispel the chilly rectitude and straitlaced priggishness found in too many children's books, however, Pyle avoided those stratagems resorted to by kindly but unskilled and essentially dishonest writers for children— sentimentality, artificial coziness, spurious charm, and deliberate sprightliness. Instead, Pyle, like Twain and Stevenson, never hesitated to show young readers a picture of life strenuous and hard, of a world where harsh reality is often masked by beguiling appearances, where duty, frequently unpleasant, leads to success, and unchanneled desire inevitably to catastrophe. Pyle's legendary heroes—Robin and Arthur, particularly—disport in Arcadia, but come eventually to admit death's universal sway even there. His folktale and historical heroes—Otto and Myles Falworth, to name only two—often must hack through the world's inhospitable thicket to a place of refuge, order, and control. Thus Pyle's balanced view of life led him to portray for children a world suffused with mirth and wonder though tainted with trial and hardship. His works for children manifest an ingratiating and infectious joyfulness tempered with refreshing candor, qualities innovative in the children's fiction of his day and still attractive in our own.

Pyle's popular works for adults share many of the conventions exploited in his fiction for juveniles. Just as Pyle had taken as his fictional frameworks the plot structures inherent in ballads and folktales and fleshed them out with appropriate permutations in his works for children, so he adapted the fictional formulas underlying the sentimental romance, the historical adventure, the mystery thriller, and the pirate tale in his works for adults. His works for both audiences evince a preference for a strong, action-packed story line and lovingly delineated, painterly settings over complex, individualized characterization. In works for children such features are apposite, even requisite, but they date his adult works, characterized as these are by conventions largely outworn, piratical and melodramatic subjects now primarily of antiquarian interest, and popular formulas mostly out of fashion today. Though they feature tense, often gripping plots and can still be read with considerable pleasure, Pyle's popular romances for adults are rooted in their time and thus make few significant claims for attention from general readers of a later era.

His decision to write these popular romances was in the making as early as 1876, when he measured his literary endeavors against the early realist works of William Dean Howells and found his own lacking. Accordingly, he allied himself with Robert Louis Stevenson, with whose romances Pyle's own are often compared. Stevenson's 1880s defense of the aesthetic validity of the romance claimed for a time impassioned adherents, but contemporary critical approval was decisively turning to novelistic realism, naturalism, formal and stylistic innovation, and psychological exploration, those planks from which the twentieth-century novel would be constructed. Thus, by the late 1890s those writers like Pyle committed to the romance were being rapidly relegated to the sublunary realm of the mere "popular writer" and their works were read, if at all, with considerable condescension by mainstream critics and students of "serious" literature. By the turn of the century the gap between "serious" and "popular" fiction had widened, and though Pyle tried with minimal success to bridge this gap with his one realist novel, *Rejected of Men*, he recognized late in life that none of his works for adults would long outlive him. With this recognition came an awareness that his literary reputation would rest upon his works for children:

My ambition in days gone by was to write a really notable adult book, but now I am glad that I have made literary friends of the children rather than older folk. In one's mature years, one forgets the books that one reads, but the stories of childhood leave an indelible impression, and their author always has a niche in the temple of memory from which the image is never cast out to be thrown into the rubbish-heap of things that are outgrown and outlived.[7]

Thus Pyle could console himself at the end of his career with the accurate realization that his tales and illustrations for young people would constitute an enduring legacy.

Notes and References

Preface

    1. *Carroll, Nesbit, Pyle* (London: Bodley Head, 1968), 210; *A Critical History of Children's Literature,* ed. Cornelia Meigs (London: Macmillan, 1953; rev. ed. 1969), 287.

    2. *Children's Literature Association Quarterly* 8 (Summer 1983):3.

    3. Zena Sutherland et al., *Children and Books,* 6th ed. (Glenview, Ill.: Scott, Foresman, 1981), 205.

    4. Charles D. Abbott, *Howard Pyle: A Chronicle* (New York: Harper & Brothers, 1925); Henry C. Pitz, *Howard Pyle: Writer, Illustrator, Founder of the Brandywine School* (New York: Bramhall House, 1965).

Chapter One

    1. "When I Was a Little Boy," *Woman's Home Companion* 39 (April 1912):5.

    2. Pyle to Edith Robinson, 26 March 1895, Thornton Oakley Collection of Howard Pyle Materials, The Free Library of Philadelphia.

    3. Frank C. Schoonover, "Howard Pyle," *Art and Progress* 6, no. 12 (October 1915):438.

    4. Howard Pyle, ed., *The Buccaneers and Marooners of America* (London: T. Fisher Unwin, 1891),15–16.

    5. *The Letters of N.C. Wyeth,* ed. Betsy James Wyeth (Boston: Gambit, 1971), 21.

    6. Pitz, *Pyle,* 164. For much of the information in this chapter, as well as for biographical information in subsequent chapters, I am indebted to Pitz and to Pyle's first biographer, Charles D. Abbott, *Howard Pyle: A Chronicle.*

    7. Henry Seidel Canby, *The Age of Confidence* (New York: Farrar & Rinehart, 1934), 234.

    8. Wyeth, *Letters,* 147.

    9. Quoted in Edward V. Lucas, *Edwin Austin Abbey,* 2 vols. (New York: Charles Scribner's Sons, 1921), 1:156.

    10. *The Ruby of Kishmoor* (New York: Harper 1908), 8.

    11. "When I Was A Little Boy," 103.

    12. Pitz, *Pyle,* 10.

    13. "When I Was a Little Boy," 5.

    14. Quoted in Abbott, *Pyle,* 25.

    15. Ibid., 48–49.

    16. Ibid., 59.

17. Ibid., 154.

18. Other "weapons" for winning the struggle for success include, according to Pyle, "limitless ambition of purpose" and "unquenchable enthusiasm, coupled with a determination to succeed." In addition, one must have "the gift of imagination." "When I Was a Little Boy," 103.

19. Quoted in Abbott, *Pyle,* 113.

20. Ibid., 96.

21. Ibid., 108.

22. Ibid., 183—85.

23. Quoted in Pitz, *Pyle,* 19.

24. Rowland Elzea, "Howard Pyle and Late 19th Century American Illustration," *Catalog of the Howard Pyle Collection* (Wilmington, Del.: Delaware Art Museum, 1971), 7.

25. Pitz, *Pyle,* 104.

26. Elzea, "American Illustration," 7.

27. "Concerning the Art of Illustration," *First Year Book* (Boston: Bibliophile Society, 1902), 21.

28. Quoted in Abbott, *Pyle,* 222.

29. Richard W. Lykes, "Howard Pyle, Teacher of Illustration," *Pennsylvania Magazine of History and Biography,* July 1956, 345–46.

30. Quoted in Rowland Elzea, *Howard Pyle: Diversity in Depth* (Wilmington, Del.: Delaware Art Museum, 1973), 19.

31. Lykes, "Pyle," 363.

32. *Bulletin,* 1896–97, Drexel School of Illustration, Drexel Archives, Philadelphia, Pa.

33. "A Small School of Art," *Harper's Weekly,* 17 July 1897, 711.

34. Abbott, *Pyle,* 158.

35. *A Catalogue of Drawings Illustrating the Life of Gen. Washington and of Colonial Life* (Wilmington, Del.: John M. Rogers, 1897), 2.

36. Quoted in Pitz, *Pyle,* 136.

37. Quoted in Abbott, *Pyle,* 217.

38. Ibid., 216.

39. Pitz, *Pyle,* 157.

40. Quoted in Abbott, *Pyle,* 221–22.

41. Rowland Elzea and Elizabeth H. Hawkes, eds., *A Small School of Art: The Students of Howard Pyle* (Wilmington, Del.: Delaware Art Museum, 1980), 134.

42. Lykes, "Pyle," 347.

43. Wyeth, *Letters,* 21, 394.

44. Quoted in Abbott, *Pyle,* 125.

45. "When I Was a Little Boy," 103.

46. Quoted in Abbott, *Pyle,* 241–43.

Chapter Two

1. For the title and critical frame for this chapter I am indebted to T. S. Eliot's "Tradition and the Individual Talent," *The Sacred Wood,* 7th ed. (London: Methuen & Co., 1950).

2. Ibid., 50.

3. *A Canon of Children's Literature,* Children's Literature Association (pamphlet, n.d.). "A list of those works published before 1970 which were of major literary merit and/or possessed excellent illustration, and which the committee felt should be known by every adult specializing in the study of literature for children."

4. Joseph Ritson, *Robin Hood: A Collection of All the Ancient Poems, Songs, and Ballads,* 2 vols. (London: T. Egerton, 1795), xi.

5. R. B. Dobson and J. Taylor, *Rymes of Robin Hood* (Pittsburgh: University of Pittsburgh Press, 1976), 198–99.

6. Ibid., 58.

7. *The Merry Adventures of Robin Hood* (1883; reprint, New York: Dover Publications, 1968), vii-viii; hereafter page references to this edition cited in parentheses in the text.

8. Maurice Keen, *The Outlaws of Medieval Legend,* 2d ed. (Toronto: University of Toronto Press, 1977), 127.

9. *Harper's Young People,* 9 and 16 January 1883.

10. *Robin Hood,* vol. 2, ballad 2. Subsequent volume and ballad numbers in Ritson will be indicated in the text.

11. Ibid., 15.

12. Ibid., 1: v.

13. See John Fraser, *America and the Patterns of Chivalry* (Cambridge: Cambridge University Press, 1982) and Mark Girouard, *The Return to Camelot: Chivalry and the English Gentleman* (New Haven: Yale, 1981) for discussions of the Arthurian revival in America and Britain.

14. Quoted in Girouard, *Return to Camelot,* 256.

15. Abbott, *Pyle,* 127.

16. Ibid.

17. Sidney Lanier, *The Boy's King Arthur* (New York: Scribner's, 1880); Mary Macleod, *The Book of King Arthur* (London: Gardner, Darton, & Co., 1900); Uriel W. Cutler, *Stories of King Arthur* (New York: Thomas Y. Crowell, 1904).

18. Abbott, *Pyle,* 128.

19. See *Malory: Works,* ed. Eugene Vinaver, 2d ed. (London: Oxford University Press, 1971), 9. The passage begins "Now shall ye assay" and ends ". . . I wote wel ye are of an hyher blood than I wende ye were."

20. Abbott, *Pyle,* 127.

21. *The Story of King Arthur and His Knights* (1903; reprint, New York: Dover Publications, 1965), 23; hereafter page references to this edition cited in parentheses in the text.

22. Cutler, *Stories of King Arthur,* xvii.

23. Abbott, *Pyle,* 128.

24. Girouard, *Return to Camelot,* 180.

25. Abbott, *Pyle,* xiv.

26. Ibid., 130.

27. *Life on the Mississippi, The Writings of Mark Twain,* vol. 9 (New York: Harper & Brothers, 1903), 347.

28. Quoted in *Howard Pyle: Diversity in Depth,* 8.

29. Pyle was certainly aware of Chaucer's "Wife of Bath's Tale" as well.

30. Pitz, *Pyle,* 79.

31. Abbott, *Pyle,* 168.

32. *The Story of the Champions of the Round Table* (1905; reprint, New York: Dover Publications, 1968), 20; hereafter page references to this edition cited in parentheses in the text.

33. *The Mabinogion,* trans. Lady Charlotte Guest (New York: E. P. Dutton & Co., 1906).

34. *The Story of Sir Launcelot* (1907; reprint, New York: Charles Scribner's Sons, 1935), 166; hereafter page references to this edition cited in parentheses in the text.

35. *The Story of the Grail and the Passing of Arthur* (1910; reprint, Charles Scribner's Sons, 1938), vii; hereafter page references to this edition cited in parentheses in the text.

Chapter Three

1. J.R.R. Tolkien, *Tree and Leaf* (Boston: Houghton Mifflin Co., 1965), 43.

2. Quoted in Abbott, *Pyle,* 96.

3. George MacDonald, *At the Back of the North Wind* (New York: Macmillan, 1964), 186.

4. *Pepper & Salt* (New York: Harper & Brothers, 1886), vii; hereafter page references to this edition cited in parentheses in the text.

5. Charles D. Abbott notes in his biography that Pyle always found "the verse medium unwieldy" (103).

6. *The Garden Behind the Moon* (New York; Charles Scribner's Sons, 1895), 82.

7. Tolkien, *Tree and Leaf,* 32.

8. *The Wonder Clock* (1888; reprint, New York: Dover Publications, 1965), v; hereafter page references to this edition cited in parentheses in the text.

9. Tolkien, *Tree and Leaf,* 26.

10. Roger Sale, *Fairy Tales and After* (Cambridge: Harvard University Press, 1978), 225. I am indebted to Roger Sale for the title of this chapter.

11. Bruno Bettelheim, *The Uses of Enchantment* (New York: Knopf, 1976), 76, 24.

12. Ibid., 60.

13. Tolkien, *Tree and Leaf,* 58–59.

14. Ibid., 65–66.

15. Ibid., 68.

16. Pitz, *Pyle,* 71.

17. *Twilight Land* (1895; reprint, New York: Dover Publications, 1968), 1; hereafter page references to this edition cited in parentheses in the text.

18. Tolkien, *Tree and Leaf,* 84.

19. Pitz, *Pyle,* 77; Abbott, *Pyle,* 108.

20. Northrup Frye, *The Secular Scripture* (Cambridge: Harvard University Press, 1976), 53.

21. *A Modern Aladdin* (New York: Harper & Brothers, 1892), 110; hereafter page references to this edition cited in parentheses in the text.

22. Quoted in Abbott, *Pyle,* 110.

23. *The Price of Blood* (Boston: Richard G. Badger & Co., 1899), 13; hereafter page references to this edition cited in parentheses in the text.

24. Pitz, *Pyle,* 100.

25. *The Garden Behind the Moon;* hereafter page references to 1895 edition cited in the text.

26. Quoted in Abbott, 198.

27. George MacDonald, *The Golden Key,* illus. by Maurice Sendak (New York: Farrar, Straus & Giroux, 1967), 57.

28. Perry Nodelman, "Howard Pyle and the Adolescence of American Children's Literature" and "Pyle's Sweet, Thin, Clear Tune: *The Garden Behind the Moon,*" *Children's Literature Association Quarterly* 8 (Summer 1983): 2, 25 (Howard Pyle Commemorative Issue).

Chapter Four

1. H. S. Canby, *The Age of Confidence: Life in the Nineties* (New York: Farrar & Rinehart, 1934), 191, 199.

2. F. L. Mott, *Golden Multitudes: The Story of Best Sellers in the United States* (New York: Macmillan, 1947), 213, 211.

3. Canby, *Age of Confidence,* 200.

4. Gillian Avery, *Childhood's Pattern* (London, Hodder & Stoughton, 1975), 194, 166.

5. John G. Cawelti, *Adventure, Mystery, and Romance* (Chicago: University of Chicago Press, 1976), 35–36.

6. *Otto of the Silver Hand* (1888; reprint, New York: Dover Publica-

tions, 1967), 1; hereafter page references to this edition, cited in parentheses in the text.

7. Pitz, *Pyle,* 82, 84.

8. Quoted in Abbott, *Pyle,* 118.

9. Paul Zweig, *The Adventurer* (New York: Basic Books, 1974), 34–36.

10. *Men of Iron* (New York: Harper & Row, 1919), 1; hereafter page references to this edition cited in parentheses in the text.

11. Zweig, *Adventurer,* 91.

12. Pitz, *Pyle,* 87.

13. *Within the Capes* (New York: Charles Scribner's Sons, 1899), 1, 257; hereafter page references to this edition cited in parentheses in the text.

14. Zweig, *Adventurer,* 89, 91.

15. Cawelti, *Adventure, Mystery, and Romance,* 16.

16. *The Rose of Paradise* (New York: Harper & Brothers, 1888), 1; hereafter page references to this edition cited in parentheses in the text. Captain Charles Johnson (Daniel Defoe), *A General History of the Robberies and Murders of the Most Notorious Pyrates* (facsimile reprint, 1724 ed.; New York: Garland Publishing, 1972).

17. Zweig, *Adventurer,* 246, 227.

18. *The Story of Jack Ballister's Fortunes* (New York: Century Co., 1895), 365; hereafter page references to this edition cited in parentheses in the text.

19. *The Buccaneers and Marooners of America* (London: T. Fisher Unwin, 1891), 15; hereafter page references cited in the text.

20. *Stolen Treasure* (New York: Harper & Brothers, 1907), 42; hereafter page references cited in the text.

21. *Howard Pyle's Book of Pirates,* comp. Merle Johnson (New York: Harper & Row, 1921; reprint, 1949). "Blueskin the Pirate" and "Captain Scarfield" originally appeared in *The Northwestern Miller.* Hereafter page references to the *Book of Pirates* cited in the text.

22. *The Ruby of Kishmoor* (New York: Harper & Brothers, 1908), 8-9; hereafter page references cited in the text.

23. Quoted in Abbott, *Pyle,* 188.

24. *Rejected of Men* (New York: Harper & Brothers, 1903), v; hereafter page references cited in the text.

25. Abbott, *Pyle,* 194.

Chapter Five

1. Pitz, *Pyle.*

2. Abbott, *Pyle,* xiii.

3. Ibid., xiv.

4. Ibid.

5. Israel Shenker, "The Plover and the Clover and Dover," *New York Times Book Review,* Part 2 (7 May 1972), 6; John Rowe Townsend, *Written for Children* (Philadelphia: J. B. Lippincott Co., 1965), 148.

6. From the prefaces to *Pepper & Salt* and *The Merry Adventures of Robin Hood.*

7. Quoted in Abbott, *Pyle,* 131.

Selected Bibliography

PRIMARY SOURCES

Publication information concerning certain rare first editions and simultaneous publication in England was taken from *Howard Pyle: A Record of His Illustrations and Writings,* compiled by Morse and Brincklé.

The Garden Behind the Moon. New York: Scribner's; London: Lawrence & Bullen, 1895.

Men Of Iron. New York: Harper; London: McIlvane, 1892.

The Merry Adventures of Robin Hood. New York: Scribner's; London: Sampson, Low, Marston, Searle & Rivington, 1883. Reprint. New York: Dover, 1968.

A Modern Aladdin. New York: Harper, 1892.

Otto of the Silver Hand. New York: Scribner's; London: Sampson, Low, Marston, Searle & Rivington, 1888. Reprint. New York: Dover, 1967.

Pepper & Salt. New York: Harper, 1886.

The Price of Blood. Boston: Badger, 1899.

Rejected of Men. New York: Harper, 1903.

The Rose of Paradise. New York: Harper, 1888.

The Ruby of Kishmoor. New York: Harper; London: Harper, 1908.

Stolen Treasure. New York: Harper, 1907.

The Story of the Champions of the Round Table. New York: Scribner's; London: Newnes, 1905. Reprint. New York: Dover, 1968.

The Story of the Grail and the Passing of Arthur. New York: Scribner's; London: Bickers, 1910.

The Story of Jack Ballister's Fortunes. New York: Century, 1895; London: McIlvane, 1897.

The Story of King Arthur and His Knights. New York: Scribner's; London: Newnes, 1903. Reprint. New York: Dover, 1965.

The Story of Sir Launcelot and His Companions. New York: Scribner's; London: Chapman, 1907.

Twilight Land. New York: Harper; London: McIlvane, 1895. Reprint. New York: Dover, 1968.

Within the Capes. New York: Scribner's, 1885.

The Wonder Clock. New York: Harper; London: McIlvane, 1888. Reprint. New York: Dover, 1965.

SECONDARY SOURCES

Abbott, Charles D. *Howard Pyle: A Chronicle.* New York: Harper, 1925. The standard biography, with an introduction by N.C. Wyeth. The only source for some of Pyle's personal and professional correspondence.

Children's Literature Association Quarterly 8 (Summer 1983). "Howard Pyle Commemorative" edition, marking the publication centennial of *The Merry Adventures of Robin Hood.* Various critical essays on Pyle's life, career, and works.

Elzea, Rowland, et al. *Howard Pyle: Diversity in Depth.* Wilmington, Del.: Delaware Art Museum, 1973. An exhibition catalog dividing Pyle illustrations into seven categories.

Lykes, Richard W. "Howard Pyle: Teacher of Illustration." *Pennsylvania Magazine of History and Biography,* July 1956, 339–70. Analysis of Pyle's teaching objectives and methods.

Morse, Willard S., and Gertrude Brincklé. *Howard Pyle: A Record of His Illustrations and Writings.* Wilmington, Del.: Wilmington Society of the Fine Arts, 1921; reissued, Detroit: Singing Tree Press, 1969. Complete bibliography of writings and illustrations.

Nesbitt, Elizabeth. *Howard Pyle.* London: Bodley Head, 1966. An introductory monograph surveying Pyle's life and work.

Pitz, Henry C. *The Brandywine Tradition.* Boston: Houghton, Mifflin, 1969. Places Pyle in a tradition of Brandywine Valley artists and illustrators.

Pitz, Henry C. *Howard Pyle: Writer, Illustrator, Founder of the Brandywine School.* New York: Bramhall House, 1965. Complete biographical and critical survey, especially strong in assessing Pyle's career as illustrator and teacher. Includes a generous sampling of Pyle illustrations.

Pyle, Howard. "When I Was a Little Boy." *Woman's Home Companion* 39 (April 1912): 5, 103. Autobiographical reminiscence attributing his success to lessons learned in childhood.

Wyeth, Betsy James, ed. *The Wyeths: The Letters of N. C. Wyeth, 1901–1945.* Boston: Gambit, 1971. A contemporary portrait of Pyle as man and teacher by his most gifted student.

COLLECTIONS OF HOWARD PYLE MATERIALS:

The Howard Pyle Collections. Delaware Art Museum, Wilmington, Del.

The Thornton Oakley Collection of Howard Pyle Materials. Free Library, Philadelphia, Pa.

Index